WORLD WAR I BATTLES

ESSENTIAL LIBRARY OF
WORLD WAR I

Essential Library

An Imprint of Abdo Publishing
abdopublishing.com

BY NEL YOMTOV

CONTENT CONSULTANT

JASON MYERS, PHD
INDEPENDENT SCHOLAR

abdopublishing.com

Published by Abdo Publishing, a division of ABDO, PO Box 398166, Minneapolis, Minnesota 55439.

Printed in the United States of America, North Mankato, Minnesota

092015
012016

Cover Photo: Bettmann/Corbis/AP Images
Interior Photos: Bettmann/Corbis/AP Images, 1; Everett Historical/Shutterstock Images, 4, 7, 22, 30, 44, 54, 74, 76, 78, 89, 90, 93, 98 (top), 98 (bottom), 99 (top), 99 (bottom); Bain News Service/Library of Congress, 13, 14, 35, 53; Daily Mirror/Mirrorpix/Corbis, 19; Red Line Editorial, 25; AP Images, 26, 47; Virginia Mayo/AP Images, 29; FPG/Hulton Archive/Getty Images, 36; Haeckel Collection/Ullstein Bild/Getty Images, 40; National Photo Company Collection/Library of Congress, 51; The Print Collector/Heritage Images/Glow, 57, 60, 87; Culture Club/Getty Images, 62; Harris & Ewing/Library of Congress, 67, 84; Lebrecht Music & Arts/Corbis, 68; Bettmann/Corbis, 82

Editor: Melissa York
Series Designers: Kelsey Oseid and Maggie Villaume

Library of Congress Control Number: 2015945647

Cataloging-in-Publication Data

Yomtov, Nel.
World War I battles / Nel Yomtov.
p. cm. -- (Essential library of World War I)
ISBN 978-1-62403-927-0 (lib. bdg.)
Includes bibliographical references and index.
1. World War, 1914-1918--Campaigns--Juvenile literature. 2. Battles--History--20th century--Juvenile literature. I. Title.
940.4/1--dc23

2015945647

CONTENTS

Tanks were an unexpected and terrifying weapon when they first appeared in battle during World War I.

SEEDS OF DISCONTENT

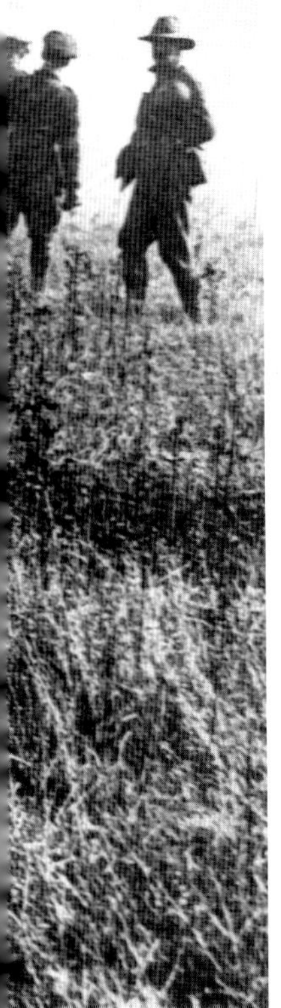

Dawn. September 15, 1916. Bert Chaney, a 19-year-old soldier in the British army, awoke from a restless night's sleep in the muddy trench he and his companions called home. Chaney's outfit was stationed near the Somme River in northern France. Enemy German soldiers were positioned in a small village called Flers, located on the other side of a wide, rubble-filled field.

Suddenly, Chaney and his mates were startled by the sound of strange throbbing noises coming from behind them. They whirled around to see what looked like two huge mechanical monsters advancing their way. The young soldiers had never seen anything like them before.

The strange vehicles were the new weapons Bert had heard about—British tanks. The soldiers sat in stunned silence as the iron giants rumbled across the field toward the German-occupied village. Without warning, the tanks began firing their machine guns, which were mounted on both sides of each vehicle. The bullets tore into the wood and brick buildings of the village where the German soldiers were positioned.

The tanks pushed down walls and flattened everything that stood in their way. As they did, the British commander ordered Chaney and his companions into the village. There, they overwhelmed the German troops and took hundreds of prisoners.

Chaney had witnessed the birth of a new battlefield weapon—the armored tank. This powerful fighting machine would come to dominate all future wars. Yet it will always be remembered for making its debut on the bloody battlefields of World War I (1914–1918).

A WORLDWIDE TRAGEDY

World War I, also known as the Great War, was fought on a scale never before known or imagined. It was the first truly world war, fought by more than 65 million soldiers from five continents—from North America to Asia. Roughly 8.5 million soldiers, sailors, and airmen were killed, and 21 million were wounded.[1] Another 5 million civilians are estimated to have died from warfare, hunger, and disease.[2]

The Great War was tremendously damaging to both people and landscapes.

The four years of brutal fighting changed the world in cataclysmic ways. The great, sprawling empires and monarchies of Europe—Russia, Germany, and Austria-Hungary—were shattered and replaced by new forms of government. The Ottoman Empire was defeated and split apart, giving birth to new nations in the Middle East. The United States, which entered the war late, began its rise as an international superpower.

In combat, the Great War was a conflict of firsts. It was the first war to make use of chemical weapons, such as the poison gases chlorine and mustard gas. Mass bombings of civilian populations from aircraft occurred for the first time. Tanks made their first appearance, thundering across battlefields throughout Europe.

Some historians call World War I a "tragic and unnecessary conflict."[3] Could the worldwide tragedy that toppled governments and caused millions of deaths have been avoided through diplomacy? After all, diplomacy had settled quarrels between these very same warring nations in the recent past. Why didn't diplomacy work this time? What events thrust the world's leading powers to the edge of conflict—and then further, into the chaos of bloody combat?

AMBITIONS, FEARS, AND ALLIANCES

Historians often view the year 1870 as the starting point of major hostilities between the powerful nations of Europe. In that year, France—fearful of a unification of independent German states—declared war on several of those states. The better-trained and larger German army quickly defeated the French. France was forced to turn over to Germany its northeast provinces of Alsace and Lorraine, which lay on Germany's western border.

Otto von Bismarck, the German chancellor, used the victory to establish the German Empire. In the years following the war, German industry boomed. As Germany gained industrial power, it began competing with other European nations, including France, for overseas trade markets.

Russia, too, had dreams of expansion, especially in the Balkans, a large region of southeast Europe. Russia viewed itself as the protector of Serbia, a Slavic nation wishing to free itself completely from the influence of Austria-Hungary.

Austria-Hungary was a union of the Empire of Austria and the Kingdom of Hungary. Many of its inhabitants were Slavic minorities, such as Serbs, who resented Austrian rule.

By the eve of war in 1914, Europe was divided into two major alliances. Nations in each alliance agreed to come to the aid of their partners should the parties be threatened by military aggression. Germany, Austria-Hungary, and Italy formed the Triple Alliance. The United Kingdom, France, and Russia came together to form the Triple Entente, also known as the Allies.

Rival governments glorified their military strength and whipped up patriotic passions and distrust of other countries. Europe was caught in the grip of fear, national pride, honor, and the alliances each nation had entered.

THE ARMS RACE

Europe's mounting tensions and rivalries led to a military buildup across the continent. France increased its army from 611,000 to 850,000 between 1912 and 1913, and Germany's army grew similarly. Other countries also increased military spending from 1900 until the war.[4]

Fearful of war with the United Kingdom, Germany began a program of building a navy to surpass the powerful British fleet. The United Kingdom—which had been the world's dominant naval force for 100 years—responded by engaging Germany in a naval arms race.

THE ASSASSINATION OF ARCHDUKE FERDINAND

On June 28, 1914, Gavrilo Princip, a 20-year-old Serbian man, shot and killed Archduke Franz Ferdinand, the heir to the throne of Austria-Hungary, and his wife, Sophie. Princip was trained in terrorism by the Black Hand, a secret Serbian nationalist organization that was dedicated to freeing Slav lands from Austrian rule.

Austria-Hungary and its emperor, Franz Joseph, believed Serbia was responsible for the assassination. On July 23, Austria-Hungary delivered demands to Serbia. The ultimatum called for Serbia to permit Austrian agents to oversee an investigation into the assassination, among other demands. Serbia refused. However, hoping to avoid armed conflict, Serbia suggested they negotiate with the help of the Great Powers. Austria-Hungary refused, and, confident of German

NEWSPAPER REPORT OF THE ARCHDUKE'S ASSASSINATION

The assassination of Archduke Franz Ferdinand made the newspaper headlines around the world. On June 29, 1914, the *New York Times* front page blared, "Heir to Austria's Throne Is Slain with His Wife by a Bosnian Youth to Avenge Seizure of His Country." The story continued, "Two pistol shots were fired in quick succession by an individual who called himself Gavrilo Princip. . . . The motor car in which they [the Archduke and his wife] were seated drove straight to the Konak [Building], where an army Surgeon rendered first aid, but in vain. Neither the Archduke nor the Duchess gave any sign of life."[5]

support, declared war on Serbia on July 28. From then on, events unfolded like falling dominoes.

THE ROAD TO RUIN

Upon Austria-Hungary's declaration of war on Serbia, the German fleet began mobilizing for armed service. The next day, July 29, a partial mobilization of Russian soldiers and artillery was heading toward the border with Austria.

That day, Austrian riverboats began bombarding Belgrade, Serbia. Russia, although considering itself Serbia's self-appointed protector, wanted to avoid war with Germany. The Russian emperor, Czar Nicholas II, appealed directly to Germany's Kaiser Wilhelm II. The two men were third cousins and had been writing each other letters for many years.

"To try and avoid such a calamity as a European war," wrote Nicholas, "I beg you in the name of our old friendship to do what you can to stop your allies from going too far."[6] The czar signed his telegram "Nicky."

"I am exerting my utmost influence to induce the Austrians to deal straightly to arrive at a satisfactory understanding with you," read Wilhelm's reply.[7]

But it was too late. When news of Russia's partial mobilization reached German military leaders, the Germans mobilized their army in response. On July 30, the czar ordered full mobilization of his Russian troops.

Germany next turned to France and demanded it remain neutral in the growing tensions. France refused and ordered a mobilization on August 1. That day, Germany declared war on Russia, and Russia responded in kind. Two days later, the Germans declared war on France.

On August 3, Germany demanded that Belgium allow German troops to move freely through the country so they could attack France. The United Kingdom warned the Germans not to cross into Belgium. The British were honoring the Treaty of London of 1839, which bound them to protect Belgium's neutrality in the event the tiny nation was attacked. But on August 4, German troops stormed into the tiny nation of Belgium. Hours later, the United Kingdom declared war on Germany. Within eight days, the Austrians declared war on Russia, and the United Kingdom and France declared war on Austria-Hungary.

Much of Europe was now at war: the British, French, and Russian Empires aligned against the empires of Germany and Austria-Hungary. Many European nations eyed the brewing storm from the sidelines: the Ottoman Empire, Portugal, Greece, and others refused to take sides at this time. Italy, despite its partnership in the Triple Alliance, declared neutrality. In May 1915, Italy would declare war on Austria-Hungary and enter the conflict on the Allies' side. Europe was on the road to ruin. Within days, several million soldiers from across the continent were on the move.

KAISER WILHELM II

1859–1941

Wilhelm II, the German kaiser, or emperor, was one of the key figures of World War I. During his birth on January 27, 1859, a doctor accidentally damaged the newborn's left arm, and it grew to be about six inches shorter than his right arm. Some historians believe Wilhelm made up for the disfigurement with an unusually strong interest in the army, the navy, and military uniforms. Wilhelm succeeded his father in 1888. Germany's new ruler was arrogant, impulsive, and easily angered. His political decisions led German chancellor Otto von Bismarck to predict Wilhelm would destroy Germany.

To this day, historians argue Wilhelm's role in the war. Some claim he did not want war but was instead controlled by his generals. Others say he held substantial political power, and as commander-in-chief of the German army, he could have prevented the conflict from erupting.

The German army used howitzers and other large artillery pieces to roll through Belgium.

1914: STORM CLOUDS BREAK

On August 4, 1914, German cavalry and infantry soldiers crossed into Belgium. Their first objective was to smash through a ring of 12 forts protecting the city of Liège. After storming through the tiny country, German forces would then invade France from the north. The Germans considered the relatively small Belgian army to be insignificant and easily defeatable. After facing early Belgian resistance at the fortress city, on August 8, the Germans began bombarding the forts with mighty cannons. On August 16, the last of the forts surrendered.

The Germans rapidly swept west through Belgium and captured Brussels, the capital. The remaining portions of the Belgian army evaded capture and retreated north to the city of Antwerp. The German First, Second, and Third Armies continued south, smashing the heavily outnumbered French Fifth Army at the battle of Charleroi on August 22 and 23. French general Charles Lanrezac, commander of the Fifth Army, was forced to pull back across the Sambre and Meuse Rivers. But he could not count on help from the closest French unit, the Fourth Army; they were fighting for their lives in the Ardennes Forest to the south. The Germans were poised to swarm into France.

THE BATTLE OF MONS

During the fighting in Belgium, the British Expeditionary Force (BEF) was ferried across the English Channel to France. Approximately 80,000 soldiers, with their equipment and horses, had landed at various channel ports and at

THE SCHLIEFFEN PLAN

German World War I strategy was based on a plan developed by Count Alfred von Schlieffen, chief of the German General Staff between 1891 and 1905. It was designed in the event Germany had to fight a war simultaneously with France and Russia. Von Schlieffen believed France would be able to mobilize more quickly than Russia. Therefore, the majority of German forces would deal with France, while a small defensive operation would keep the Russians in check. After an estimated six-week victory over the French, vast numbers of German armies would be sent to the eastern front to defeat the Russians.

Rouen on the Seine River.[1] The BEF would travel to the front and join the left flank of General Lanrezac's Fifth Army at the Belgian-French border. Together, the Allies hoped to prevent the German armies from entering France.

Allied leadership, however, was unaware of the full nature of the threat it faced from the enemy. General Joseph Joffre, commander-in-chief of the French armies, had underestimated the number of advancing German troops. The Allies were also uncertain about the exact route German armies were taking toward the border. Based on such incorrect and incomplete information, General Joffre mistakenly placed Allied troops in a position where they could be easily attacked from the north and east by German armies. The Allied fighting was doomed from the start.

On the afternoon of August 22, the BEF entered the town of Mons, Belgium. Sir John French, commander-in-chief of the BEF, expected to form part of an offensive on the Allied left wing. But when he arrived in Mons, he learned Lanrezac's Fifth Army had been attacked the day before, and it was unable to recross the Sambre River to join the BEF.

The Fifth Army was getting pounded along its entire front. Its force at Namur, a Belgian fortress city located where the Sambre joins the Meuse, was beaten off. Meanwhile, German forces were threatening the Fifth Army on its right flank. Lanrezac asked Sir John French to attack the Germans coming at his army, but Sir John wisely refused. If he turned to assist Lanrezac, the Germans could attack him from the rear. Instead, Lanrezac retreated from his position.

It was now left for the BEF to hold a defensive line that stretched for 27 miles (43 km) along the Mons-Condé Canal—alone. The position around Mons, in particular, had several weaknesses, including poor positions to set up field artillery and inadequate protection from enemy shelling. The Germans decided to attack headlong at Mons, straight into the British lines.

FIELD ARTILLERY

Field artillery is a type of large military weapon that fires explosive shells farther than the bullets of rifles and other small arms. Much of the artillery used in the early stages of World War I had a relatively short range of 7,000 yards (6,400 m). During the war, guns increased in size and range. Some were so massive they could be moved only by specially designed heavy-duty railroad cars.

On August 23, the Germans launched the attack with a barrage of artillery, followed by charging infantry soldiers. As the German army advanced, British riflemen and machine gunners cut the attackers down in a hail of gunfire. After repeated failed attempts to crack the British line, the Germans unleashed heavy artillery and machine-gun fire on the BEF. By mid-afternoon, the British were forced from their positions and withdrew to villages south of Mons. Sir John French gave the order to cease fire, and under cover of darkness, the BEF moved out. The retreat from Mons began, and the Germans moved in to seize the village.

British cavalry retreats from Mons.

The battle of Mons was the first major action of the BEF in World War I. Although the Allies lost the battle, the orderly withdrawal from Mons was efficient and did not result in panic. The retreat lasted nearly two weeks, taking the BEF to the outskirts of Paris. There, combined British and French forces would launch a historic counterattack at the battle of the Marne in September.

BATTLE OF TANNENBERG

As the French battled German troops storming through Belgium, Russia agreed to help distract the Germans with an offensive in German East Prussia. On August 17, the Russian First Army, under General P. K. Rennenkampf, invaded East Prussia. Three days later, the Russian Second Army, under A. V. Samsonov, also crossed the border. The two armies were to meet up and attack the German Eighth Army from the east and south, roughly 50 miles (80 km) apart. Initially, the Russian attack went well, as the First Army defeated the Germans at Gumbinnen on August 20. Separated by huge distances, however, the two Russian armies were unable to communicate their movements to each other—a situation that would prove deadly.

After intercepting an uncoded radio message revealing the Russians' plans, German commanders Paul von Hindenburg and Erich Ludendorff jumped into action. On August 26, the Germans surprised Samsonov's army near the village of Tannenberg, in present-day Poland. For three days, German artillery pounded Samsonov's troops, forcing the Russians to retreat. As the Russians pulled back, German forces met them, and a large-scale massacre followed. Within days, the Germans had taken 92,000 prisoners and crushed the Russian Second Army.[2]

The Germans next turned on Rennenkampf's First Army, driving it from East Prussia by mid-September. In all, the Russians lost approximately 250,000 men and untold amounts of military equipment.[3] The Allies, however, tried to find comfort in one aspect of the battle: Russia's defeat at Tannenberg had tied up German troops in the East, allowing the French to counterattack at the Marne.

BATTLE OF THE MARNE

On the western front—the area of fighting west of Germany—the German armies pursued the BEF as the British retreated southward after the battle of Mons. The Germans, however, faced several problems of their own. They had to send troops to fortify Belgium, especially Antwerp, and the French towns of Givet and Maubeuge. The loss of personnel convinced the Germans they did not have the manpower or time to attack and seize Paris, the capital of France.

EARLY AIR RECONNAISSANCE

Early in the war, military leaders became convinced of the value of air reconnaissance to get a broader view of the battlefield, using aircraft including the airplane, which was barely a decade old. At the first battle of the Marne, General Joseph-Simon Gallieni used information from British air reconnaissance to launch a successful counterattack against the Germans. At the battle of Tannenberg on the eastern front, General Samsonov ignored warnings about German troop strength and movement, which ultimately led to his army's destruction. German leaders at the same battle used their knowledge of Russian troop movements to devastating effect. "Without airmen there would have been no Tannenberg," said victorious German field marshal Paul von Hindenburg.[4]

French soldiers shelter in a ditch awaiting German attack during the battle of the Marne.

Instead, the Germans would continue moving south and pass to the east and southeast of Paris. There, they would strike the French armies and destroy them. On September 3, however, British air reconnaissance revealed the German First Army was not moving toward Paris but instead had turned southeast toward Compiègne.

Upon learning of the Germans' plan, Joseph-Simon Gallieni, military governor of Paris and commander of the Paris Army, convinced French military leaders the time had come to launch a counteroffensive. On September 3, the

German First Army, in pursuit of the BEF, reached the Marne River. The Germans did not believe the French would launch a major counterattack, but they were wrong. The next day, General Joffre approved Gallieni's plan for a full-scale operation against the invaders.

On September 6, the French Sixth Army, commanded by Michel-Joseph Maunoury, launched an infantry and cavalry attack against the right flank of the German First Army from the direction of Paris. The Germans put up stiff resistance but retreated to positions west of the Ourcq River. Gallieni rushed in French reinforcements, including as many as 6,000 soldiers who arrived at the front in taxicabs![5]

To meet the threat of Maunoury's Sixth Army, the German First Army was forced to turn westward. During the maneuver on September 7 and 8, the First Army became separated from the Second Army. This opened a gap of approximately 30 miles (50 km) between the two armies—an invitation to disaster for the Germans. On September 9, the BEF and the French Fifth Army poured into the gap, threatening widespread destruction of the German armies. The Germans retreated, but the Allies' lack of fresh troops prevented them from crushing the enemy entirely.

By September 12, the Germans had retreated behind the Aisne River. There, they dug a line of trenches along the heights of the Chemin des Dames Ridge,

600 feet (180 m) behind the Aisne. The stage would be set for one of the war's most famous military operations—the Race to the Sea.

THE BATTLE OF THE AISNE AND THE RACE TO THE SEA

On the night of September 13, the BEF and French troops crossed the Aisne River to attack the entrenched German armies. But as they approached the German positions, they were raked by German gunfire. Neither Germans nor Allies could move the other, but neither side would retreat. The next day, the Allies began digging trenches for protection using tools taken from nearby farms and villages.

As days wore on, the Germans kept the Allies pinned down and inflicted heavy damage. German howitzers lobbed huge shells into the Allied trenches, while German troops used mortars and grenades with deadly accuracy. The Allies lacked heavy weapons, and the artillery they did possess were no match for the Germans' artillery in range and numbers.

The armies were at a standstill. Both sides gave up the idea of waging frontal assaults on the other. To break the deadlock, each combatant made a series of unsuccessful maneuvers to outflank the other, in what has become known as the Race to the Sea. Neither side was really trying to reach the North Sea, but rather sought to outflank their opponent by going north. Major battles were fought

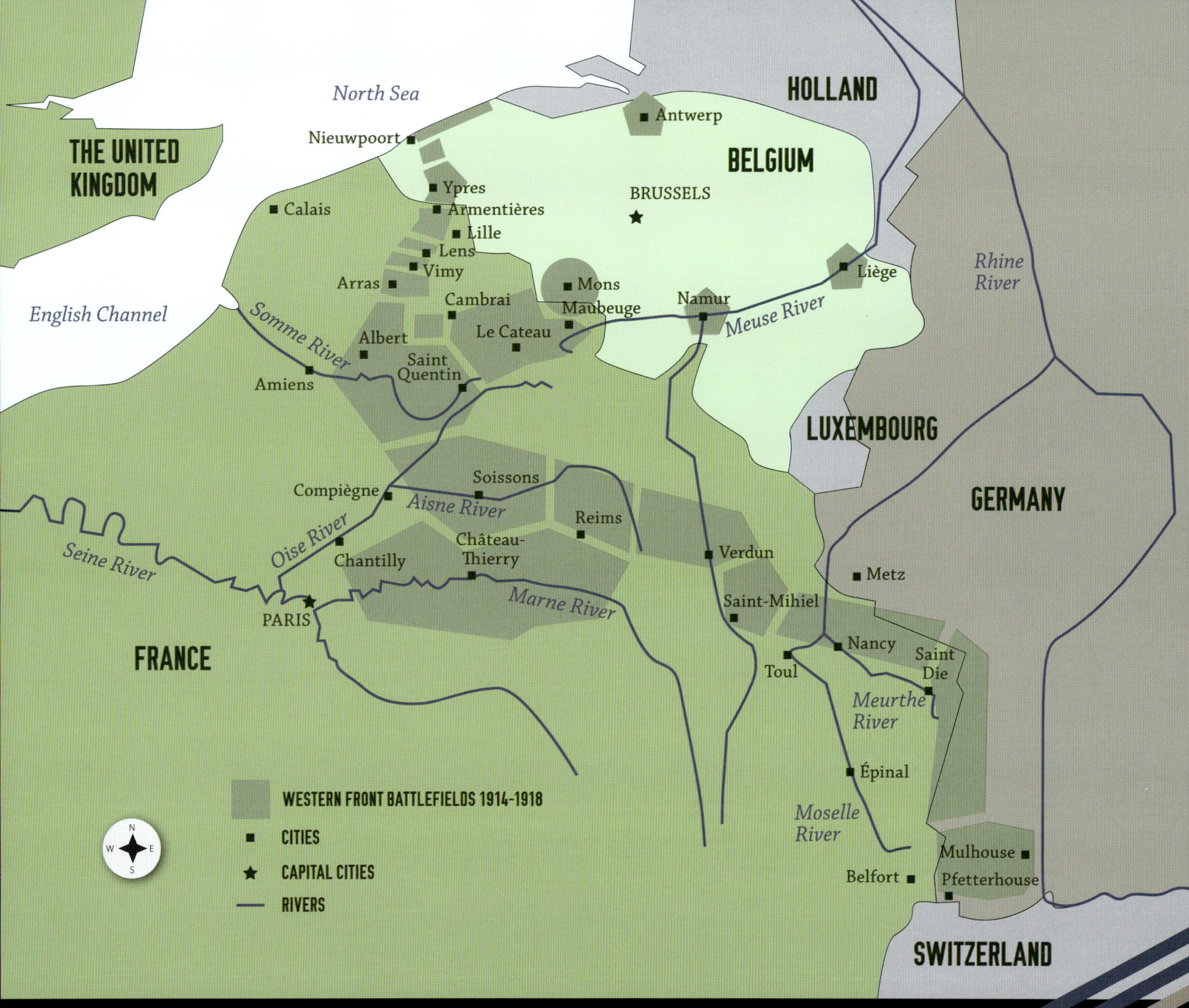

The western front

Battlefield conditions grew increasingly uncomfortable as autumn turned to winter in 1914.

near the Somme in late September and then Arras in early October. In early October, Lens and Armentières were the sites of large-scale fighting.

The final phase of the Race to the Sea ended with the first battle of Ypres in Belgium, fought from October 19 to November 22. The Germans wanted control of Ypres because of the network of roads that ran in and out of the town. For nearly four weeks, the battle seesawed back and forth, with the Germans making territorial gains only to lose them to Allied counterattacks. Once again, the fighting ended in a stalemate.

In all, German, British, and French casualties at the first battle of Ypres were nearly 250,000. Germany alone suffered roughly 130,000 dead and wounded.[6]

As 1914 drew to a close, so did the first phase of the Great War. Despite the horrendous loss of life, neither side held the upper hand. The system of opposing trenches on the western front now stretched more than 400 miles (640 km), from the Alps in southeast France to the North Sea. For three and a half years, the lines would advance only ten miles (16 km) in either direction.

TRENCH WARFARE

The battle of Ypres marked the transition from a war of moving infantry soldiers to a war of fixed trench lines. By the end of 1914, trenches had become a major factor in the fighting. At first, the trenches were simple burrows in the ground dug to the depth of an average soldier's height, offering simple protection from enemy gunfire. The front of the trench was further protected by barbed wire to discourage the enemy from surging into the trench. Trenches were constructed in zigzagging lines to prevent the enemy from having an open line of fire down long stretches of a trench.

Most armies built three lines of trenches. The first was the front line, closest to the fighting zone. If the enemy overran the first trench, the army would fall back and occupy the support trench 250 feet (75 m) back. Approximately 1,000 feet (300 m) behind was the reserve trench, where troops would gather for a counterattack if the first two trenches were overrun.

As the months wore on and the stalemate continued, trenches were more sturdily built. Sandbags, wooden slats to walk upon, and wooden or concrete sides were placed in the trenches. Some German trenches even featured carpets, brass bed frames, and other luxuries.

Daily life in the trenches was dangerous and primitive. Any movement above the trench line drew deadly rifle fire from enemy snipers. Trenches were easy targets for artillery shells, grenades, and trench mortars, which fired shrapnel, bombs, and canisters of poisonous gas.

Rats, frogs, and lice infested trenches year-round. Feeding on human remains, brown rats could grow to the size of a cat. The rats spread disease and contaminated

Trenches varied widely in their comfort levels.

the soldiers' food. Lice lived in the men's dirty clothing, causing itching and trench fever, a disease marked by severe pain and high fever. Tens of thousands of soldiers suffered trench foot, an infection of the feet caused by wet and unclean trench conditions. Many cases of trench foot resulted in amputation.

For more than four years, the combatants at the front endured these gruesome conditions. It is estimated as many as one-third of all Allied casualties on the western front were suffered in the trenches.[7]

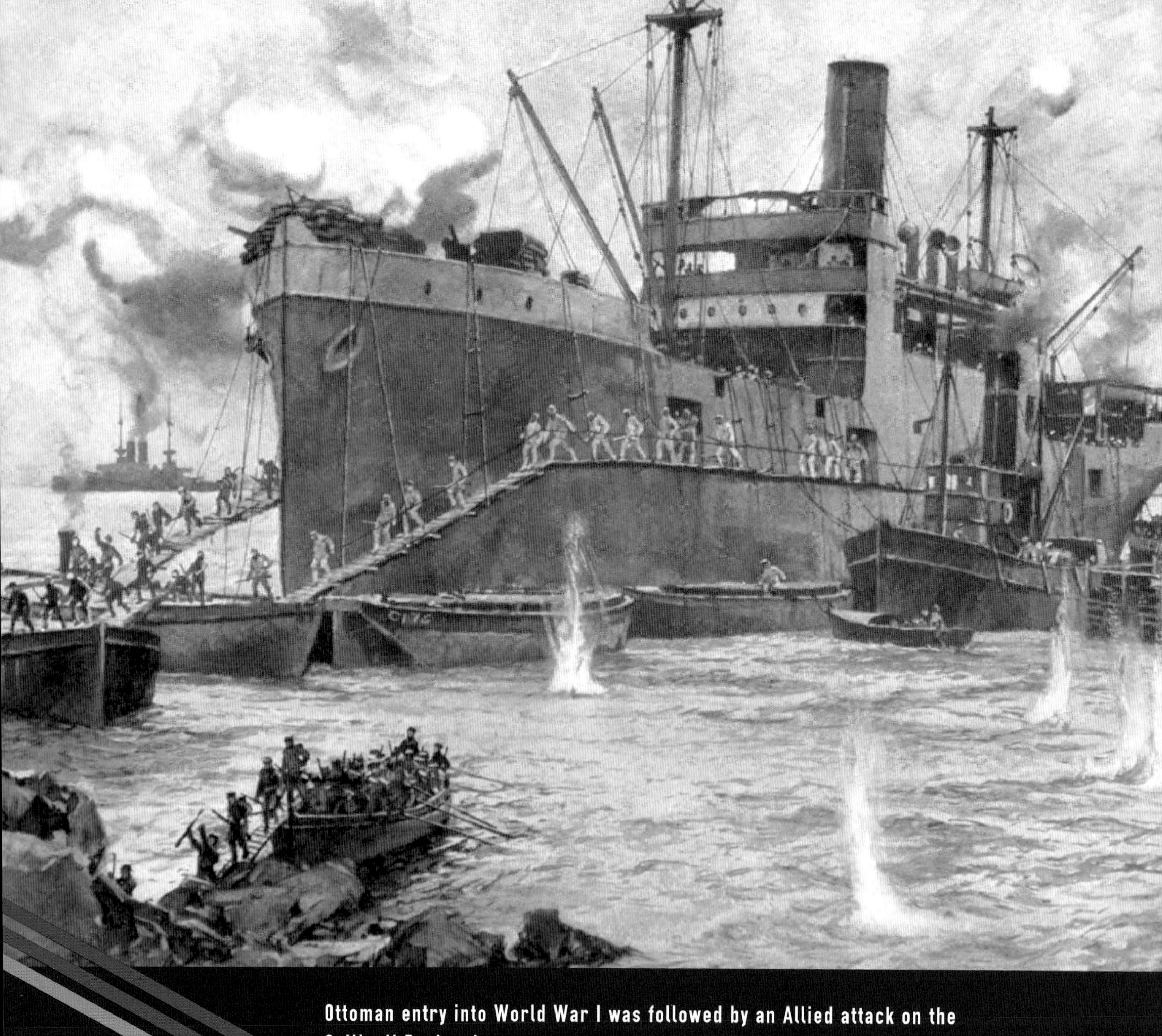

Ottoman entry into World War I was followed by an Allied attack on the Gallipoli Peninsula.

1915: THE CONFLICT SPREADS

By the dawn of 1915, it was clear the Great War would not soon be over. The stalemate in the trenches along the western front promised a long-term war. In addition, the entry of other nations into the conflict began extending the fighting outside Central Europe. One key development occurred in August 1914, when Enver Pasha, the Ottoman Empire's minister of war, signed a treaty with the German ambassador. The Ottoman Turks had sided with the Central powers.

THE GALLIPOLI CAMPAIGN

The Dardanelles is a narrow, 40-mile- (64 km) long strait that connects the Aegean Sea in the Mediterranean with the Sea of Marmara. The Sea of Marmara leads to the Black Sea, where Russia's southern ports were located. The Dardanelles separates the Gallipoli Peninsula of European Turkey from Turkey in Asia. In January 1915, Russian armies were battling Ottoman Turks in the Caucasus Mountains at the border of Europe and Asia. The Russians needed relief and requested assistance from their allies.

A SUBMARINE AT GALLIPOLI

On April 25, the HMAS *AE2* submarine of the Royal Australian Navy secretly slipped into the Dardanelles strait as part of the Gallipoli campaign while ANZAC troops landed on the beaches. For the next several days, *AE2* cruised the Sea of Marmara, making several unsuccessful attacks against Turkish ships. On April 30, *AE2* spotted the Ottoman torpedo boat *Sultanhisar*. The submarine dove and went to investigate. One mile from the Turkish boat, *AE2* rose to the water's surface. While attempting to dive back under, the *Sultanhisar* fired on the submarine, blasting its hull in several places. *AE2*'s commander ordered the crew to evacuate. The submarine sunk in only a few minutes. The *Sultanhisar* captured the entire crew of the submarine. The *AE2* lay unseen until 1998, when a team of archaeologists using a high-definition camera spotted it at the bottom of the Sea of Marmara.

The idea appealed to the British and French: a successful operation at the Dardanelles, they believed, could lead to the eventual capture of Constantinople, the capital of the Ottoman Empire. The Turks, anticipating a possible Allied assault, placed hundreds of explosive naval mines in the straits.

Between February 25 and March 14, British warships bombarded Turkish forts on the Dardanelles and landed marines on the peninsula to destroy Turkish artillery. But the Allies were unable to clear the mines from the straits. On March 18, the British navy tried again to smash through the strait. Of the 16 battleships sent into action, three were sunk and three badly damaged by Turkish heavy artillery.[1] None of the ships reached the minefields.

The solution to the dilemma was to land troops to knock out the Turkish artillery positions. This would allow Allied minesweeping vessels to clear out the mines in the strait without fear of attack from Turkish guns. British warships would then be free to sail where the mines had been cleared.

The plan was to assemble 70,000 men—mostly soldiers of the Australian and New Zealander Army Corps (ANZAC)—and dozens of ships at the Greek island of Lemnos.[2] This landing force would sail from Lemnos and land on the Gallipoli Peninsula. Delays in loading the ships and organizing the soldiers, however, gave the Turks plenty of time to reinforce their troops.

Nevertheless, on April 25, the first Allied landing party was put ashore on the peninsula. The operation was a disaster from the beginning. The first wave of ANZAC troops landed at the wrong place. The troops reorganized and began advancing toward the high ground of Sari Bair. Turkish forces under the leadership of Mustafa Kemal, however, halted the ANZAC advance. Over the next several months, approximately 50,000 Allied soldiers would die in unsuccessful attacks on the hilltops in the region.[3]

Meanwhile, British forces were landing at Cape Hellas, the tip of the Gallipoli Peninsula, at five different beaches. The Allied attack stalled, pinned down by thousands of Turkish forces that had moved up to push back the landing. Immediately, troops on both sides began digging lines of trenches, just as the men had done on the western front. For the next several months, the deadlocked troops endured a brutally hot summer and freezing early winter. Men died from disease and ill-fated attacks and counterattacks.

To break the deadlock, British general Sir Ian Hamilton planned a new assault at Suvla Bay, west of the original landing beaches. It seemed like a good spot for a surprise attack: Suvla Bay was defended by a force of only 1,500 Turkish troops, supported by a few howitzers but no machine guns.[4]

The invasion was conducted on the night of August 6. Lacking adequate maps and leadership, however, some of the men landed in the wrong places, and others wandered the beaches aimlessly. Mustafa Kemal rushed reinforcements to the area. Once again, the Allies were pinned in along the peninsula's beaches—and again the attackers and the defenders dug into trench positions.

MUSTAFA KEMAL

1881–1938

Mustafa Kemal was the hero in the Turkish defense of the Gallipoli Peninsula. After World War I, he began a nationalist revolution to resist the occupation and splitting of the Ottoman Empire after its defeat in the war. In 1919, he became leader of the Turkish War of Independence, fighting against the armies of Greece, Armenia, France, the United Kingdom, and Italy. After leading his forces to victory in 1922, the Turkish mainland was completely liberated from Allied control and the Ottoman Empire was abolished. In October 1923, the Republic of Turkey was proclaimed and Mustafa Kemal was elected its first president. The new leader launched a series of progressive reforms to modernize Turkey, including increased independence for women and the introduction of Western legal codes. In 1935, he was given the surname Atatürk, meaning "father of the Turks."

Turkish troops repelled the invaders at Gallipoli.

By late autumn, British leaders realized the situation at Gallipoli was hopeless and planned for a withdrawal of the armies. From December 1915 through January 8, 1916, British troops withdrew, ignored by the Turks who were unaware a full evacuation was underway. The devastation at Gallipoli was appalling: approximately 300,000 Turkish men were dead, wounded, or missing. The Allies suffered 265,000 casualties.[5]

SECOND BATTLE OF YPRES

For much of 1915, the Gallipoli campaign used Allied soldiers, supplies, and other resources that were badly needed on the western front. The situation distressed Sir John French, commander-in-chief of the BEF. Meanwhile, General Joseph Joffre, commander of the French armies, announced his plans to launch an offensive. Sir John agreed to relieve the French armies positioned near Ypres. In early April, he took over five miles (8 km) of French trenches northeast of the city. With men tied up in Gallipoli, however, Sir John had no idea when much-needed reinforcements would arrive.

At 5:00 p.m. on April 22, German artillery zeroed in on the small town and unleashed a 20-minute nonstop bombardment. When the men in the trenches, four miles (6 km) east of Ypres looked to the skies, they saw two greenish-yellow clouds gradually merging into one. The odd-looking cloud floated toward the trenches and swept over the men, bringing slow death, painful paralysis, and unimaginable terror to more than 15,000 soldiers.[6]

The cloud was poisonous chlorine gas. It was the first use of the gas in World War I. With no protection against the attack, the gas burned and choked the men and destroyed their lungs. Some men saved themselves by using their shirts or handkerchiefs as makeshift masks. Many died on the spot. The lucky ones who managed to escape the cloud fled in horror.

A German bombardment with standard artillery shells continued throughout the night. Meanwhile, the Allies' Canadian Division waged brutal attacks and counterattacks against the enemy. Amid the confusion, German infantrymen finally swarmed toward Ypres, reaching to within 2,500 yards (2,300 m) of the town. Innocent civilians, including children, ran from their homes in panic. But soldiers from Canadian and British divisions halted the German attack.

Although the battle lasted officially from April 22 to May 25, fighting at the second battle of Ypres continued for months. Both sides suffered heavy losses. British casualties numbered approximately 60,000, while the Germans had 35,000 dead, wounded, and missing.[7]

Colonel Henri Mordacq, an officer with the French Forty-Fifth Division, was an eyewitness to the war's first use of chlorine

GAS ATTACKS

After the war's first use of gas at Ypres on April 22, 1915, both sides commonly used gas warfare. In September 1915, at the battle of Loos, the British used chlorine gas for the first time. That summer, the Germans began using phosgene, which caused a delayed reaction, striking victims down 24 hours later. Mustard gas was particularly harmful, causing blisters on the skin and eye and respiratory damage. Gas could easily blow back against the troops who deployed it, too. Early protection used by the Allies was simply water-soaked handkerchiefs, rags, and towels. Later, gauze pads soaked in special solutions and placed over the mouth and eyes were used. Until the end of the war, goggles, flannel hoods, and different types of masks, including those with screw-on filters, were issued to the soldiers.

gas. “The scene was more than sad; it was tragic,” he wrote. “It was no longer soldiers who were escaping but poor souls who had become suddenly insane.”[8]

The year 1915 ended inconclusively. The Central powers seemed to have the upper hand on both the western and eastern fronts. The Germans had halted every attempt by the French and British to smash the trench line and had dealt their enemies heavy losses. In the east, the Germans had beaten the Russians at major battles, while the Ottoman Turks had won a tremendous victory at Gallipoli. However, the fighting power of the French, British, and Russian armies had not been destroyed. In addition, the Western allies seized control of Germany’s colonies in Africa. The year of 1916 would be a time of great battles both on land and on the sea, as the combatants made the big push toward victory.

ITALY JOINS THE CONFLICT

On May 23, 1915, Italy—which had until this time remained neutral—declared war on Austria-Hungary. Although they had been a formal member of the Triple Alliance, the Italians watched the war unfold from the sidelines, carefully considering on whose side they would fight, if either. Eventually, Italy decided to join on the side of the Allies based on the conditions of the Treaty of London, signed in 1915. By its terms, Italy would receive control over land on its border with Austria-Hungary, among other territorial gains. Italy’s entry into the conflict opened a new front—the Italian front—stretching 370 miles (600 km) along Italy’s border with Austria-Hungary.

Chief of General Staff Erich von Falkenhayn, *right*, met with Archduke Friedrich of Austria-Hungary, *left*, at German headquarters in 1915.

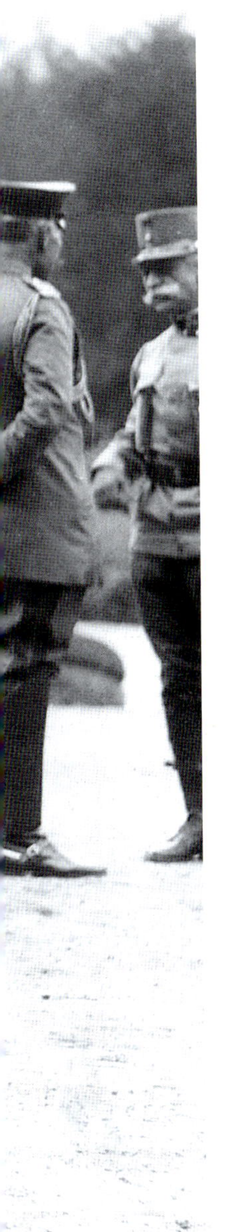

1916: THE BIG PUSH

The Germans were encouraged by their successes on the eastern front in 1915. A major battle at Masurian Lakes in present-day Poland resulted in 56,000 Russian casualties and 100,000 prisoners.[1] Yet the Russians stubbornly refused to lay down their arms, forcing Germany to wage war on two fronts. Chief of General Staff Erich von Falkenhayn was convinced Germany and its allies could not continue fighting indefinitely: they needed to go on the offensive and win the war in the coming year. Believing the French were incapable of bearing the burdens of war for much longer, von Falkenhayn planned a major offensive, intended to "bleed France white."[2]

BATTLE OF VERDUN

The city of Verdun was a symbol of national pride for the French. Located in northeastern France, Verdun had been a historically important—although not strategic—military site for centuries. Von Falkenhayn planned to crush the French army at Verdun with an overwhelming artillery assault, thereby crushing the national spirit of France.

Verdun was surrounded by a series of forts. The forts had been strengthened with concrete but did not have enough artillery guns. When the bombardment ended, a small German infantry force would advance on the French line and push the remaining army from the battlefield. If necessary, the process would be repeated.

The Germans moved more than 1,200 guns of all types and sizes to a three-mile (4.8 km) front east of the Meuse River, due north of Verdun.[3] The Germans not only had a four-to-one advantage in artillery but also greatly outnumbered the French army. The assault by the German Fifth Army was originally planned for February 12, 1916, but a blizzard prevented the action. The French used the delay to improve their fortress defenses.

On February 21, the Germans fired the first devastating shot of the battle, hitting the cathedral in Verdun nearly 20 miles (30 km) away. For nine hours, the bombardment continued, constantly growing ever more fierce. French soldiers were buried alive in their trenches as mountains of exploded soil, trees, and debris rained down upon them. Damaged machinery, dead animals, and human bodies lay scattered all around. Railroad links to Verdun were destroyed, cutting off the town's supply line.

It is estimated the Germans fired approximately 80,000 shells during the assault.[4] When the bombardment stopped, nearly 140,000 German soldiers began moving toward the French line, carrying with them a fearsome weapon: the flamethrower.[5] The French soldiers fought stubbornly and inflicted heavy casualties on the enemy, but they could not hold back the Germans.

The Germans repeated the procedure again and again, and on February 25, they seized control of the fort at Douaumont, the greatest of the forts protecting Verdun. Panic spread through the streets of the city. French troops were in disorder, and

FLAMETHROWERS IN WORLD WAR I

The first important use of flamethrowers in World War I came in a German attack on British forces in Belgium in July 1915. The weapon, called a *Flammenwerfer*, was designed to ignite flammable oil. Once lit, the oil was shot from a hose, resulting in a stream of fire and clouds that traveled nearly 20 yards (18 m). The Flammenwerfer device was strapped to the back of one man, who directed the hose with the assistance of a companion. Flamethrowers were used mainly to clear out trenches and drive enemy defenders from the battlefield. The British designed several models of flamethrowers in preparation for the battle of the Somme, fought in July 1916. By 1917, the French had developed a one-man flamethrower, using it primarily in trench attacks until the end of the war.

Flamethrowers inflicted frightening destruction during World War I.

huge traffic jams of military vehicles clogged the roadways. Verdun seemed on the edge of collapse.

In the last days of February, French general Philippe Pétain was put in command of the entire area's defense. Rallying his soldiers under the battle cry "They shall not pass!," Pétain organized his troops and established a roadway for trucks to bring supplies to the front, especially artillery guns.[6]

Fighting continued throughout March and April, with each side attacking and counterattacking again and again. The ruins of the tiny village of Vaux changed hands 13 times during March. Battles were waged to the east and west of Verdun, both north and south of the Meuse River.

By late June, both sides combined to fire an estimated 23 million shells in four months. The entire landscape was devastated: forests destroyed, villages in ruins, and the earth ravaged by the endless shelling. “Humanity . . . must be mad to do what it is doing,” a young French lieutenant wrote in his diary on May 23. “What scenes of horror and carnage! . . . Hell cannot be so terrible.”[7]

The Germans attempted a final offensive on July 11, but it was turned back. From then on, both sides adopted a defensive position, and on October 24, the French recaptured the fort at Douaumont. In December, the battle officially ended with French armies recapturing most of the ground lost on the east bank of the Meuse. The human loss was staggering: roughly 750,000 men had been killed, wounded, or lost in action.[8] By then, action on the western front had shifted to the Somme River.

THE BATTLE OF JUTLAND

The Allies called it “Jutland” and the Central powers “Skagerrak.” It was not only the largest naval battle of the war but of naval history up to that time. The event featured the world’s two most powerful naval fleets: the British Grand Fleet under Admiral Sir John Jellicoe and the German High Seas Fleet, commanded by Admiral Reinhard Scheer.

Admiral Jellicoe led a massive fleet: 28 battleships, nine battle cruisers, eight armored cruisers, 26 light cruisers, and 78 destroyers. Admiral Scheer commanded 22 battleships, five battle cruisers, 11 light cruisers, and 61 destroyers and flotilla leaders.[9]

German submarines were a deadly threat to Allied ships of all types in the region. In late May 1916, the British learned through intercepted German radio messages that German U-boats, or submarines, were moving to a position somewhere off the English coast. On May 30, the British sent two fleets out in search of the U-boats. One fleet sailed from Scapa Flow in Scotland under Admiral Jellicoe. The second fleet set out from Rosyth, Scotland, commanded by Vice-Admiral Sir David Beatty.

On May 31, 1916, the German High Seas Fleet sailed northward from Jade Bay in Germany. Admiral Scheer's plan was to lure part of the British fleet into the North Sea near the Skagerrak, a strait running between Norway and Denmark. Scheer was unaware, however, that the British were intercepting and decoding German battle plans and knew the movements of the German fleet.

In the early afternoon of May 31, British and German ships came in sight of each other. The British fleet under Beatty opened fire in the late afternoon, and within 60 minutes, German shells tore into four British battle cruisers. The *Tiger* and *Lion* were badly damaged, while the *Indefatigable* was sunk with 1,017 men aboard and the *Queen Mary* went down with nearly 1,300 crewmen.[10]

Admiral David Beatty's flagship, the *Iron Duke, right,* leads the *Tiger* and the rest of the fleet to the battle of Jutland.

As evening approached, Beatty's battered fleet sailed northward toward Admiral Jellicoe's fleet. The Germans pursued, and the fighting continued, finally ending after midnight.

Although both sides claimed victory, the British had taken the worse beating. Fourteen British ships had been sunk, and nearly 7,000 British sailors lost their lives. Eleven German ships were sunk, with just over 3,000 lives lost.[11] The costly encounter, however, disheartened the German fleet. For the rest of the war, it never again challenged the British Grand Fleet on so large a scale.

SUBMARINE WARFARE

Between 1915 and 1918, Germany waged on-and-off unrestricted submarine warfare against the Allies, sinking any ship without warning. German U-boats often attacked Allied shipping, hoping to prevent soldiers, food, raw materials, and supplies from reaching their destinations. Sometimes sailors or passengers from neutral nations died in German submarine attacks. On May 7, 1915, the British passenger liner *Lusitania*, sailing from New York, was torpedoed and sunk off the coast of Ireland. Twelve hundred people lost their lives, including 124 Americans.[12] Additional German attacks on passenger ships occurred later that year. Public opinion of neutral nations turned sharply against Germany. The Germans agreed to halt unrestricted submarine warfare, but the damage had already been done: anti-German sentiment, especially among the Americans, was on the rise.

THE BATTLE OF THE SOMME

In December 1915, Allied military leaders had agreed to launch a large-scale offensive on the western front the following year. French commander-in-chief Joseph Joffre and Field Marshal Douglas Haig, who had replaced Sir John French as commander of the BEF, selected the Somme River in northern France as the site of the operation. The Somme is a quiet, shallow waterway bordered by marshes that flows westward into the English Channel. With large numbers of French troops tied up fighting at Verdun, the British would be responsible for most of the action at the Somme.

On June 24, preparing for the main attack, an Allied artillery bombardment opened on the German line with nearly 3,000 British and French guns. Haig believed the ferocious attack would destroy German defenses and allow Allied troops—numbering nearly 750,000 men—to overrun the German front lines.[13] The bombardment continued for eight days but failed to destroy the German line. Many of the shells fired by the British did not go off. And German troops

IN THE EAST: THE BRUSILOV OFFENSIVE

Aleksey Brusilov, the newly appointed commander of the southern Russian front, was eager to deal the Austro-Hungarians a knockout blow. Brusilov's plan was to attack along a 200-mile- (320 km) wide front to prevent the enemy from massing reserves at any single critical spot.

The opening Russian artillery bombardment on June 4 took the Austro-Hungarians off guard. In many places, Austro-Hungarian troops had dug trenches 20 feet (6 m) deep. When Russian forces swooped upon them after the artillery assault, the men were trapped in their deep burrows and could do nothing but surrender. By mid-June, the Austro-Hungarian Fourth Army had lost 60,000 men and the Seventh Army was nearly annihilated, losing more than 100,000 troops. By the end of the month, Brusilov's troops had advanced 60 miles (96 km) in some areas of the front, seized 350,000 prisoners, and captured more than 700 pieces of artillery.[14] They pushed farther into Austria-Hungary throughout August and September. But in the end, unable to quickly bring supplies and reserves to the front, the Russian assault ground to a halt. The Russians paid a heavy price, losing more than 1 million men in the campaign.[15]

The Brusilov Offensive was Russia's first major victory—and the nation's finest hour in World War I. It would be its last: back home, Russia was tottering on the edge of political revolution.

took shelter in the well-built concrete bunkers they had constructed in the months prior to the attack.

The Allied ground attack began on July 1. Expecting little or no opposition, British troops slowly walked toward the German lines carrying their weapons and supplies. The highly skilled German machine gunners easily mowed them down. By the end of the day, the BEF had suffered 57,000 casualties, including approximately 20,000 dead.[16] However, Haig continued the attack in the following days.

On July 11, British forces captured the first line of German trenches. The Germans responded by bringing in troops from Verdun to shore up the defense at the Somme. The fighting continued for months, with Haig and the German High Command each convinced the other side was at its breaking point.

On September 15, British tanks attacked German lines at the battle of Flers-Courcelette, the first major use of tanks in the war. Forty-nine Mark I tanks were to take part in the battle. Due to mechanical difficulties, however, only 31 tanks crossed the German lines, and only nine tanks were able to lead the British infantry's advance.[17] The tanks were unreliable and difficult to maneuver. During the fighting, some of the tanks mistakenly fired on their own infantry.

Despite British advances in the later stages of the campaign, the Allied Somme offensive came to a halt on November 18. In four months of fighting, the British and French had gained only 7.5 miles (12 km) of ground—at a cost

French workers with the Red Cross, an international medical and humanitarian organization, help soldiers wounded during the battle of the Somme.

of 420,000 British casualties and 200,000 French casualties. German casualties numbered at least 500,000.[18] There was no clear winner at the Somme—and the western front remained frozen in a stalemate.

In August 1916, German commander Paul von Hindenburg succeeded Erich von Falkenhayn as chief of the German Army General Staff. The next month, von Hindenburg ordered the construction of a heavily fortified defense line to be built five to 30 miles (8 to 40 km) behind the western front. It was to run between the north coast of France and Verdun, near the border between Belgium and France. The aim of the Hindenburg Line was to halt any Allied breakthrough before it could approach the Belgian or German frontier. The newly built defensive zone would play a major role in the events of 1917.

TANK WARFARE

The Mark I tank used at the Somme held a crew of eight men. An officer and the driver sat up front; a gunner and his mate sat in each compartment on either side of the vehicle; and two mechanics worked the gears that turned the tracks. The tank was covered with armor 0.25 to 0.5 inches (0.6 to 0.12 mm) thick and equipped with one small gun in each side compartment and three machine guns. The tank carried 324 rounds of ammunition for each side gun. Early tanks, such as the Mark I, however, were unreliable and difficult to maneuver across the battlefield. The United Kingdom's first successful, large-scale use of the tank occurred at the battle of Cambrai in November 1917. The notable performance of British tanks at Cambrai encouraged the US and German armies to quicken production of their own models.

TANK PRODUCTION OF THE MAJOR COMBATANTS IN WORLD WAR I[19]

YEAR	UNITED KINGDOM	FRANCE	GERMANY	UNITED STATES
1916	150	-	-	-
1917	1,277	800	-	-
1918	1,391	4,000	20	84

British Mark I tank

The complex German system of trenches made their positions nearly impossible to attack.

1917: THE CRITICAL YEAR

In the spring of 1917, Robert Nivelle, commander-in-chief of the French Army, led a major offensive to break through the German defenses on the Aisne River. The attack began on April 16 with a combined force of 1.2 million French and British troops.[1] The offensive had failed by mid-May, with 40,000 French soldiers dead on April 16 alone.[2] The devastating French loss at the second battle of the Aisne led to widespread mutiny among French troops. Philippe Pétain, the French hero of Verdun, was named to replace Nivelle.

THE BATTLE OF MESSINES RIDGE

By June 1917, German forces had been dug in along Messines Ridge, a stretch of high ground just south of Ypres, for more than two years. From this vantage point, the Germans overlooked British positions, which they could bombard almost at will. The Germans had fortified the Belgian villages of Messines and Wytschaete as well as the surrounding woods, farmhouses, and cottages. A network of trenches, concrete shelters, pillboxes, artillery batteries, and barbed-wire defenses made up the German front line. The position was nearly impenetrable.

The Allies' aim was to capture the higher ground of the ridge to increase their strategic advantage in the region. Preparations for a battle began in early 1916, when British general Herbert Plumer ordered Allied engineers to dig 22 tunnels into the ridge, under the German lines. Huge mines were to be placed in the tunnels, totaling more than

GERMAN PILLBOXES: MINI FORTRESSES

The Germans found it difficult to dig trenches along the high ground in areas of the western front. Instead, they built concrete blockhouses, called pillboxes, from which troops fired upon the enemy. The boxes were so solidly constructed that only a direct artillery hit could destroy them. Pillboxes also offered the troops inside protection from the weather. Machine gunners stationed in the boxes fired their weapons through narrow openings. The German High Command discovered that because several men served together in the small box, their comradeship and morale remained high.

Miners dig under Messines Ridge to breach the German defenses.

one million pounds (450,000 kg) of explosives. The Germans discovered one tunnel and destroyed it. The British decided not to use two others.

At 3:10 a.m. on June 7, the British set off the remaining 19 mines. The effect of the enormous explosions on the Germans was devastating: 10,000 men were immediately killed.[3] The blast was so loud it was heard hundreds of miles away.

The Allies quickly swarmed upon the shaken German troops with a barrage of artillery, tanks, and gas attacks. Within three hours, the first line of German defense had fallen. At 7:00 a.m., the Allies attacked again but were met with stiff resistance. Germans fired from the doorways and windows of the farmhouses and cottages and hurled grenades from behind walls. Machine gunners blasted at the attackers from cellars and concrete pillboxes.

By late morning, Messines and Wytschaete had fallen. The Allies took 7,000 German prisoners, nearly 300 machine guns, and dozens of artillery pieces and trench mortars.[4] By 5:00 p.m., Allied troops had seized all of their objectives. They dug in. German troops launched a counterattack the next day, but they were beaten back, and the Allies gained even more ground. By June 11, the Germans had started withdrawing and were setting up a new front farther east.

Despite heavy losses, the Allied victory at Messines boosted morale among the soldiers. It also perked up the spirits of Allied civilians, who were growing increasingly weary of the war. Due to a lack of forces, however, Commander-in-Chief Haig was unable to quickly follow up on the success at Messines. Instead, he began preparing for a major breakthrough at Passchendaele the following month.

THE THIRD BATTLE OF YPRES AND PASSCHENDAELE

Commander Haig believed relentless, repeated attacks on the Germans would drive them to the point of collapse. He hoped to rapidly follow up the success achieved at Messines with a swift assault on German positions at Ypres. It took

RUSSIA'S REVOLUTION

As a result of demonstrations and uprisings by workers, peasants, and elements of the Russian army, Russian czar Nicholas II was forced from power on March 15, 1917. On July 1, the new government, led by Alexander Kerensky, launched the Kerensky Offensive against Austro-Hungarian and German troops in Galicia on the eastern front. After initial Russian success, German counterattacks inflicted heavy damage on the attackers. By July 16, the advance collapsed completely. The provisional government was weakened by the failure of the operation. On November 7, the Bolshevik Party (later the Communist Party) seized power in the Russian capital, Moscow, and declared its desire to end Russia's participation in the war. On December 15, the Russians agreed to an armistice with the Germans, which was formally signed in early 1918. Russia was out of the war. Tens of thousands of German troops were now available for service on the western front.

time, however, to move thousands of troops and guns and millions of shells toward the battle site.

The German defenses at Ypres consisted of a series of well-fortified lines. A thinly manned forward line ran along Pilckem Ridge, with a second line behind it on the opposite slope. Behind this were more lines rising up to Passchendaele Ridge. Concrete pillboxes and farm buildings, housing German machine gunners, covered the area. The German strategy was to slow down enemy attacks and cut down survivors with fierce counterattacks from beyond the range of British artillery.

Soldiers hide in a machine gun nest.

In an attempt to soften German defenses, an Allied bombardment began on July 18, 1917. For more than two weeks, 3,100 guns fired more than 4.5 million shells.[5] Given the intensity of the attack, the Germans fully expected a large-scale offensive, so the Allies lost the element of surprise. Worse, the shelling tore up the rain-soaked ground, creating fields of huge water-filled craters Haig's troops would need to cross.

The British assault began on August 4, with troops moving forward in a heavy fog. They took three ridges on the German left flank, but on the right, German resistance halted progress. Then came the rains. Endless downpours turned the field into a huge mud pit. Soldiers sank into the muck up to their thighs, while tanks were barely able to move at all. But Commander Haig remained confident of victory. The rains continued for another two weeks, preventing the British from mounting a second assault.

When the grounds at last became somewhat passable, the Allies resumed the attack on August 16. Once again, they made small gains on the left flank but halted on the right. The gains came during four days of intense fighting at the village of Langemarck, during which the British suffered heavy casualties and the town itself was reduced to rubble. British morale sagged.

Commander Haig placed General Herbert Plumer—the mastermind of the mine tunnels at Messines—in charge of conducting a series of small, well-organized assaults on the Germans, rather than a single, full breakthrough. At battles fought on September 20 and 26 and October 4, Plumer established British control of the southern end of the Passchendaele Ridge, east of Ypres. These limited gains, however, cost the Allies many lives, and the operation overall was a failure. But Haig pressed on, ordering attacks on the German-controlled part of Passchendaele Ridge for October 9 and 12.

Soldiers battled through deep mud during the third battle of Ypres.

At the battle of Poelcappelle on October 9, the Allies suffered huge losses of men, mostly New Zealand troops, in mud and heavy downpours. On October 12, Australian and New Zealander forces took a fierce beating. Unwilling to admit failure, Haig launched three more attacks in late October. Progress was small and losses very high. The Germans unleashed mustard gas on the exhausted Allied attackers.

On November 6, British and Canadian forces finally seized the high ground of Passchendaele. The village itself was nearly wiped out by the weeks of fighting. Haig was satisfied: he finally called off the offensive, hailing it as a great Allied success. In reality, numerous objectives beyond Passchendaele still had not been taken, nor were the Germans driven off.

The capture of the ridge came at a huge cost to the Allies, including 310,000 casualties. Approximately 40,000 men were never found, many of whom had drowned or were buried in the mud.[6] The Germans reportedly suffered 260,000 casualties.[7]

THE BATTLE OF CAMBRAI

During 1917, the British had built up its tank corps and were looking for an opportunity to use the units against the Germans. The rain-soaked, muddy fields of Passchendaele, however, were no place for tanks. By early November, Commander Haig approved a major tank-based offensive against the German lines in northern France.

The Allies chose the region of Cambrai as the site of the attack. The ground was firm, and the German positions were lightly manned, mainly because it was a relatively quiet area of the western front. Two weeks before the start of the battle, the British moved artillery units into position, while infantry units were moved up by rail and road. Many of the tanks moved into a thickly wooded area southwest of Cambrai. Others were concealed in nearby ruined buildings. By November 19, the tanks and troops were in place for the attack. To ensure complete surprise, there would be no opening artillery bombardment on the Germans.

The attack rolled out at dawn on the morning of November 20, with the tanks advancing across a six-mile (9.7-km) front. Four hundred and seventy-six Mark IV tanks streamed toward the German line, supported by infantry and cavalry divisions. As the tanks moved across the open, grass-covered field, 1,000 pieces of artillery opened fire on the Germans, their shells falling nearly 200 yards (190 m) ahead of the tanks.[8]

The Germans were caught completely off guard. Many fled in panic, while others surrendered without resistance. Approximately 8,000 German prisoners

HOW TO FIGHT A TANK

Understandably, the Germans were unprepared to fight the tanks that surprised them at Cambrai. They had no special guns or bullets to penetrate armor, but instead relied on their field artillery to blow apart the tanks. German infantry soldiers often attacked tanks with flamethrowers, hoping the fire would blind the driver as he looked through the observation window. Late in the war, the Germans developed an antitank rifle, which fired a bullet that could penetrate armor 0.86 inches (2.2 cm) thick at 330 feet (100 m). A two-man crew composed of a gunner and an ammunition carrier operated the gun.

and 100 guns were captured.[9] More important, the Germans had been pushed back six miles (9.7 km) from the front.

By November 27, the assault fizzled. Tank crews, infantry, and cavalry troops were all exhausted. On November 30, German general Georg von der Marwitz launched a fierce counterattack with enormous success. Within one week, the Germans recovered all the ground they had lost. The impressive initial breakthrough had been wasted because of the Allies' lack of reserves.

Battle casualties, as usual, were high: the British suffered losses of roughly 45,000 men, while the Germans suffered approximately 50,000.[10] Although the British had failed to achieve a lasting breakthrough, the battle of Cambrai had demonstrated the enormous potential of the tank in battlefield conditions.

ENTERING THE WAR

In the early years of World War I, both the US government and the public believed neutrality was in the nation's best interest. However, hostility toward Germany increased when a German U-boat sunk the passenger ship *Lusitania* on May 7, 1915, killing 124 Americans. Due to international outrage, the Germans stopped unrestricted submarine warfare after the incident.

On January 9, 1917, however, Kaiser Wilhelm II announced the restart of the policy. In February, US officials intercepted a message, called the Zimmerman telegram, sent from the Germans to the Mexican government offering a partnership of war against the United States. The two incidents enraged the country.

The final straw came in March when the American ships *City of Memphis* and *Illinois* were sunk by U-boats. On April 2, President Woodrow Wilson addressed the US Congress, asking its support to enter the war. "There is one choice we cannot make, we are incapable of making," he said. "We will not choose the path of submission."[11] The US Congress voted to support the president, and the country declared war on Germany on April 6. By December 1917, 175,000 American troops were in France, but no large group had yet seen battle. By the summer of 1918, nearly one million US soldiers would be in Europe, half of them in frontline action.[12]

By 1917, Woodrow Wilson saw no way to continue keeping the United States out of World War I.

The Germans quickly realized their dirigibles could drop bombs on enemy cities.

THE WAR IN THE AIR

At the beginning of World War I, both sides used aircraft mainly for reconnaissance. The usual mission of airplanes and gas-filled dirigible airships, called Zeppelins, was to fly over enemy territory and report on opposing troop strength and movements. At the time, airplanes were generally slow and had not been designed for combat. Nevertheless, airplanes were sometimes used as military weapons from the start of the war.

When hostilities erupted in August 1914, few aircraft were combat-ready. The Germans had approximately 180 planes and 20 seaplanes, aircraft capable of taking off and landing in water. The British Royal Air Service and the Royal Flying Corps combined had roughly 87 aircraft. The French possessed 136 aircraft.[1]

EARLY AIR RAIDS

During the Race to the Sea in the fall of 1914, the Germans wanted to outflank the Allies and reach the ports on the French coast of the English Channel. Once there, the Germans could cut communication lines between the British army and its home bases in the United Kingdom. German Zeppelins attacked the channel ports, dropping bombs on the docks and railroad facilities.

In response, First Lord of the Admiralty Winston L. S. Churchill—later to become the prime minister of the United Kingdom—immediately ordered airplane attacks on Zeppelin bases in Germany. Churchill's strategy of using airplanes against the slower-moving Zeppelins achieved some success, but the Germans responded quickly, with devastating results.

ZEPPELINS OVER ENGLAND

Although machine-gun fire from British airplanes could blow up the gas-filled, flammable Zeppelins, the mighty balloons could fly higher than planes. Zeppelins could also fly longer distances and carry heavier bomb loads. In addition, flying at great heights, the sound of their engines could barely be heard from the ground, so it was difficult to know when they approached.

In January 1915, Germany began launching Zeppelin air attacks on towns in eastern England. The bombing of civilian targets caused outrage throughout the Allied nations. On the night of May 31, the first Zeppelin air raid on London took place. The Germans dropped firebombs and grenades, killing seven civilians and injuring as many as 40 others.[2]

A turning point in German bombing strategy came on October 19–20, 1917, when a Zeppelin raid went horribly wrong. Eleven airships were hit by heavy winds while crossing the English Channel. The storm blew the Zeppelins across mainland Europe: one airship was shot down by French artillery over the western front; two were captured in France; and one drifted out to sea and was never found. After the failed mission, Zeppelins were used mainly to attack British ships in the North Sea.

ZEPPELIN DAMAGE

The largest raid of the war occurred overnight on September 2–3, 1916, when 14 Zeppelins attacked southeast England. The ships dropped nearly 39,000 pounds (17,700 kg) of bombs, killing four people and injuring 12 others.[3] German raids on the United Kingdom increased to 22 missions in 1916, when nearly 1,000 civilians were killed or injured.[4]

AIRCRAFT IN THE NAVY

Early in the war, the navies of all the major combatants showed interest in the use of aircraft. The United Kingdom's Royal Navy Air Service built seaplane tenders, ships that carried a few seaplanes. To take off, the planes were lowered into the water by crane over the side of the ship. At the end of their mission, they would land next to the ship and be raised back up.

The British used shipborne aircraft during the battle of Gallipoli, which they fought against the Turks in 1915. During the troop landings at Suvla Bay in August, a British pilot flying a Short 184 seaplane from the tender *Ben-my-Chree* sunk a Turkish merchant ship with a torpedo—the first-ever successful aerial torpedo attack.

The Royal Navy continually experimented with the use of planes for offensive operations. Its goal was to fly wheeled aircraft from the decks of ships—aircraft carriers—and have the aircraft land back on the deck after its flight. It set afloat the world's first aircraft carriers, but they had little impact on the war. Carrier development continued after the war, with carriers later playing a major role during naval operations in World War II (1939–1945).

AIRCRAFT AT THE BATTLES OF VERDUN AND THE SOMME

When the battle of Verdun began in February 1916, the Germans had nearly complete control of the skies, with five times as many planes as the French. At Verdun, the Germans divided the area around the battlefield into three zones. Each zone was patrolled from sunrise to sunset by a formation of three planes, most likely Fokker Eindeckers. The goal of the patrol was to prevent French observation planes from flying over German lines to gather information on German troop positions and battle plans.

DOGFIGHTS: PLANE VS. PLANE

As more planes took to the skies, pilot versus pilot combat became commonplace. At first, the usual weapons were grenades, pistols, and rifles. Some pilots even threw a brick or heavy stone at their opponents' planes, hoping to damage the fragile wings or body. In 1915, the Germans revolutionized aerial combat with a new device called an interrupter. The device allowed a pilot to fire front-mounted machine guns straight ahead without destroying his own propeller. Air fights became known as dogfights, and the best pilots were nicknamed aces, a title given to aviators who shot down five or more enemy planes. Most dogfights took place over the skies of the western front.

German pilot Kurt Wintgens was the first fighter pilot to shoot down an enemy aircraft using the new interrupter technology. On July 1, 1915, Wintgens, flying in a Fokker, downed a French pilot in a Parasol-type aircraft while fighting over the town of Lunéville in eastern France. After several minutes of combat, Wintgens wounded the French pilot in the leg, forcing him to land.

The French, however, were able to penetrate the German zones with the recently introduced Nieuport 11 single-seat fighter aircraft. By midyear, the French had considerably built up their air strength, numbering 120 planes to oppose 168 German planes.[5]

In the early fighting at the battle of the Somme, German pilots flew in formations called *Jagdstaffeln*, or "hunting packs." These groupings of 12 planes roamed the skies over the Somme, pursuing British B.E.2c observation planes. Initially, the German hunting packs had success. However, when the British

A German observer photographs the scene below from an airplane.

began using the Sopwith 1½ Strutter, their most effective long-range fighter plane to date, the Allies regained air superiority at the battle. The British used a tactic called trench strafing, in which pilots flew closely over enemy trenches, firing machine guns and dropping light bombs from their planes.

AMERICAN WINGS AT THE BATTLE OF SAINT-MIHIEL

The United States had only 250 military aircraft when the nation declared war against Germany in April 1917.[6] One year earlier, however, American volunteer pilots had begun training with the Lafayette Escadrille, part of the French Flying Corps. In addition, the US government set aside $640 million for the development of US aircraft. Nearly 700 American-produced planes were sent to France by the end of the war, although no US-built craft were ever flown in combat, likely due to their late arrival in Europe.[7] Thousands of US-built Liberty engines, however, were used in planes assembled in the United Kingdom and France. The British and French governments supplied the planes US pilots flew.

In July 1917, Lieutenant Colonel William "Billy" Mitchell was named the air planner for US military operations

THE ALBATROS

The war in the air took a swift turn when the Germans introduced their DIII Albatros in early 1917. The Albatros was an improved fighter plane with a powerful engine. In the hands of a German ace such as Manfred von Richthofen, nicknamed the "Red Baron" for the bright red planes he flew, the Albatros was a deadly killing machine. During the battle of Arras, which began on April 9, 1917, the British Royal Flying Corps (RFC), with 385 aircraft, flew in support of a massive ground offensive. Led by von Richthofen, the Germans tore into the RFC, overwhelming the Allied pilots. The British R.E.8 bomber and S.E.5 Bristol and F.2A fighters were no match for the skilled German pilots flying their Albatros. During April, the British lost 245 aircraft and had 211 airmen killed or missing—the worst casualty numbers rung up by the RFC in the war.[8]

in Europe. He helped train American pilots and established air bases in France for the growing Air Service branch of the US Army. In September 1918, Colonel Mitchell was placed in charge of planning the air campaign for the battle of Saint-Mihiel, the United States' first major mission of World War I. Mitchell assembled a combined American-British-French force of 1,476 planes—the world's largest gathering of aircraft up to that time.[9]

Mitchell devoted roughly one-third of his aircraft to support the Allied ground troops. Planes dropped light bombs and strafed enemy frontline positions with machine guns. Long-range bombers attacked German rear positions, including enemy airfields. Although the Germans

A French Spad takes down a German Albatros in a dogfight.

fought fiercely for control of the skies, relentless Allied attacks coupled with Mitchell's careful planning won the day. The battle was a huge Allied victory and marked the first time in the war that massive air support had been given to advancing ground troops. Weeks later, Mitchell would command the Air Service in support of the battle of the Meuse-Argonne, which would help bring the war to an end shortly thereafter.

AMERICAN ACE

Captain Eddie Rickenbacker was the United States' most decorated flying ace during World War I. When the United States entered the war, Rickenbacker enlisted. A former racecar driver, he proposed a flying group staffed by racecar drivers. The army rejected his suggestion, and he became a driver for army officers. With the help of Colonel Billy Mitchell, however, Rickenbacker entered pilot training. On April 29, 1918, Mitchell shot down his first enemy plane. By late September, he was named commander of the 94th Aero Squadron, one of the finest US air combat units. Overall, Rickenbacker was credited with 26 kills, or planes shot down, the most by any US pilot in World War I.[10]

A group of US infantry heads to the front in France to meet the German offensive.

1918: THE TIDE TURNS

By 1918, Austria-Hungary faced severe challenges on the home front. Food shortages and political unrest swept across the nation. In addition, many people among its diverse ethnic minority groups began believing an Allied victory would free them from Austro-Hungarian rule. With mounting losses on the battlefield, Austria-Hungary was on the verge of collapse by early 1918.

The entry of the United States into World War I in 1917 meant the Germans had to act fast in the spring of 1918. Could they crush the United Kingdom and France before the Americans had time to send in sufficient troops to affect the outcome of the war?

THE US ARMY UNIFORM AND WEAPONS

The uniform of the American soldier was made from either cotton or wool, depending on the season. It consisted of a khaki or olive drab shirt and trousers, leggings, trench shoes, a blouse coat, and a trench coat for winter use. Soldiers carried personal items—soap, a mess kit, a sewing kit, and a shaving kit—as well as meat, bacon, and small rations of sugar, coffee, and tobacco in a large field pack. Wire cutters, small shovels, and a water canteen and cup were standard equipment.

The standard US rifle was the Model 1903 Springfield .30 caliber and bayonet. Soldiers were also issued the Model 1911 Colt .45-caliber pistol with a holster and a pouch to hold ammunition. Shotguns were sometimes used to clear out enemy trenches. Standard equipment also included a helmet and gas mask, usually issued when the soldier arrived in France.

THE SPRING OFFENSIVES

German commander Erich Ludendorff decided to launch major offensives along the western front against the United Kingdom. The operation was to attack a front of roughly 50 miles (80 km). Ludendorff believed defeating the British would lead to a collapse of the French armies. With German troops flowing from the eastern front to the western front, Ludendorff held the advantage of manpower over the Allies.

On March 21, the first offensive, called the Michael Offensive, began. German artillery began pounding Allied positions on the western front between the Sensée and Oise Rivers. After two hours of nonstop shelling, Germany's infantry advanced forward. The British were overwhelmed. By nighttime, the Germans had inflicted 38,000 casualties on the enemy, including 21,000 prisoners.[1] The Germans swept forward, crossing the original Somme battlefield. By March 27, they had captured the French towns of Albert, Montdidier, and Ancre on the Allied right flank, in the south.

Having made tremendous gains, the Germans then focused on their main objective, Arras, to the north. There, on March 28, the British finally halted the German advance. Ludendorff let the operation wind down and prepared for the next offensive, the Georgette. The target would be British troops along the Lys River farther north.

The Georgette Offensive opened on April 9, with the Germans gaining nine miles (14.5 km) in the first day. The battle of Lys raged on, with the Germans forcing the British from Passchendaele Ridge and pushing them back nearly into Ypres. With the arrival of fresh French reinforcements, however, the Germans were unable to deal the Allies a decisive blow. Coupled with logistical problems and weak spots on the German flanks, Ludendorff gave up the Georgette Offensive on April 29. For the next month, fighting was light: the Germans were gearing up for another push.

On May 27, General Ludendorff launched his third major attack, the Blücher-Yorck Offensive. This time he targeted French forces positioned between the Rheims and Soissons Rivers, south of the two earlier spring offensives. Once again, the Germans crushed the enemy defenses and poured forward. By May 29, the Germans had captured the town of Soissons and were moving toward the

German generals Hindenburg, *left*, and Ludendorff, *right*, inspecting their troops

Marne River. There, they entered Château-Thierry—less than 60 miles (96 km) from Paris.

The three German offensives were the most successful operations along the western front since the start of the war. The Germans had pushed the front significantly westward, while battering the Allied armies, especially the British in northern France and Belgium. However, they paid a heavy price for their gains: the Michael and Georgette Offensives alone cost the Germans approximately

335,000 casualties.[2] Many of the German dead, wounded, and prisoners were from elite, well-trained units. Even more threatening to the Germans was the growing numbers of Americans arriving in France; by June, 300,000 US soldiers were arriving in France each month.[3]

ENTER THE AMERICANS

General John J. Pershing was the commander of the American Expeditionary Forces (AEF), the US armies in France. Pershing insisted his troops be allowed to fight as a unified American army, rather than integrating into existing Allied forces. In the interest of Allied victory, however, he gave US support to British and French commanders whenever necessary.

From May 28 to 31, in the AEF's first wartime offensive, American troops retook the German-captured village of Cantigny, France. The Americans suffered 1,600 casualties, including 100 killed.[4] On June 3, in action east of Château-Thierry, the Americans prevented the Germans from crossing the Marne River, thereby denying the enemy an advance toward Paris.

Three days later, on June 6, US Marine forces attacked German positions in Belleau Wood, an old hunting ground of approximately one square mile (2.6 sq km), located north of Château-Thierry. In the initial assault, German machine gunners who had dug in the rocky terrain of the forest shot at the Marines as they advanced. The fighting wore on for days, with the Marines

JOHN J. PERSHING

1860–1948

In 1917, President Woodrow Wilson selected General John J. Pershing to command the US troops in Europe. Pershing graduated from the US Military Academy at West Point in 1866 and was placed in the cavalry. He saw action in the Indian Wars against Apache and Sioux Native Americans. Pershing later served in the Philippine-American War (1899–1902) and the Spanish-American War (1898), and led an expedition against the Mexican revolutionary Pancho Villa in 1914. Pershing built the American Expeditionary Forces from scratch—rapidly organizing and training a force of inexperienced fighters that eventually grew to more than 1 million stationed in France. In 1919, Pershing was promoted to general. Pershing died on July 15, 1948, at the age of 88.

attacking, withdrawing, and then attacking again six times before they finally pushed the Germans out on June 26.

The Americans suffered nearly 9,800 casualties, including 1,811 killed.[5] Belleau Wood was the first of many victories that would contribute to the legacy of the US Marine Corps.

AMERICAN WOMEN IN THE NAVY AND MARINE CORPS

During the course of World War I, nearly 12,000 women enlisted in the US Navy and 305 in the Marine Corps.[6] The women held a variety of jobs, serving as clerks, typists, drivers, messengers, and couriers. Others were nurses and health-care workers. Some women enlistees worked in naval intelligence, breaking codes and handling sensitive and important information. Many navy women assembled devices used in torpedoes, while others recruited soldiers for the US armed forces. US women served in several overseas locations, including France, the United Kingdom, Hawaii, and the Caribbean.

THE ALLIES ADVANCE

In July, the Allies began a series of offensives that retook the Germans' spring gains and shattered German hopes of victory. By August 4, Allied troops had advanced 30 miles (48 km) eastward, taking thousands of prisoners. Four days later, at Amiens, a British tank-supported thrust shattered the German line over a 15-mile (24 km) length. On August 10, the French occupied Montdidier, followed by an offensive that captured Aisne Heights.

By late August, the Germans were abandoning many of their positions, especially in the north. On September 12, General John Pershing began an attack on German positions at Saint-Mihiel. With aerial support provided by Colonel

Mitchell, the attack caught the Germans in the process of retreating, resulting in a huge Allied victory. The Germans regrouped, however, and prepared for the next Allied onslaught: the Meuse-Argonne Offensive.

BATTLE OF THE MEUSE-ARGONNE

By late September, the battle line was much the same as it was throughout most of the war. The major difference was the entire new, fresh army—the AEF—on the southern flank of the western front. The southern portion of the German defensive lines protected two key railway lines that ran from Metz, Germany, to the northwest. The Allies chose the valley of the Meuse River and the Argonne Forest for their attack.

On September 26, the Allies opened with a barrage of artillery fire. The American First Army, led by General Pershing, advanced forward. It was supported on both left and right flanks by French troops. The plan was to rapidly advance ten miles (16 km), which would take the Allies through the first German lines and into the Argonne Forest. From there, the troops would take the hilltop town of Montfaucon. By early the next day, the Allies had achieved all of their objectives. But the Americans made few advances on September 27 and were forced to regroup for the next advance. Meanwhile, news from battlefields farther north announced the Allies had broken the Hindenburg Line, the last line of German defenses on the western front. The Germans were in trouble.

Americans man a large railway gun during the Meuse-Argonne Offensive.

Back at Meuse-Argonne, the Germans sensed the end was near and brought in reinforcements from other parts of their front. On October 4, German military leaders demanded the government in Germany make an offer of peace to the Allied powers. The idea was rejected. The same day, the Americans resumed their attack, but the Germans put up stiff resistance. Despite heavy casualties, by October 28, US troops had advanced ten miles (16 km). On their left, the

French had advanced 20 miles (32 km) and reached the Aisne River. The Allies kept pushing forward, capturing German defenses and numerous towns. The Germans withdrew from along the entire French-American front. The defeat of the German army was at hand.

THE FINAL DAYS: THE ARMISTICE

By the fall of 1918, Germany and its allies were on the edge of collapse. The end had come for the Central powers.

Since Bulgaria entered World War I on the side of the Central powers in October 1915, the Allies had waged campaigns against Bulgarian forces in Salonika, northern Greece, and Serbia. During the Allies' Vardar Offensive of September 15 to 29, 1918, Bulgarian forces crumbled under an overwhelming air attack. On September 30, the Bulgarians agreed to an armistice with Allied forces.

In late October, Italy faced Austria-Hungary on the Italian front. There, Italian forces beat the Austrians at Vittorio Veneto. The Austrian government was forced to end all fighting, and on November 3, Austria signed a peace agreement with the Allies. In the Middle East, British forces defeated the Turks at the battle of Megiddo in September and then seized the Ottoman cities of Damascus and Beirut. On October 30, the Ottoman Empire surrendered.

In Germany, a revolution forced Kaiser Wilhelm II from the throne in early November. The hardships of war had thrust the German population into near-desperation. Severe shortages of food and coal left most Germans hungry and cold. Public unrest was on the rise. Coupled with a mutiny in the German navy, political leaders convinced Wilhelm to give up his throne on November 9. A republic replaced the imperial government.

All that remained was the surrender of Germany. On the morning of November 11, 1918, political and military representatives from Germany, the United Kingdom, and France signed the armistice. World War I was officially over.

Crowds gathered in the streets across the United States and the world to celebrate the armistice.

World War I left millions dead and wide expanses of Europe in ruins.

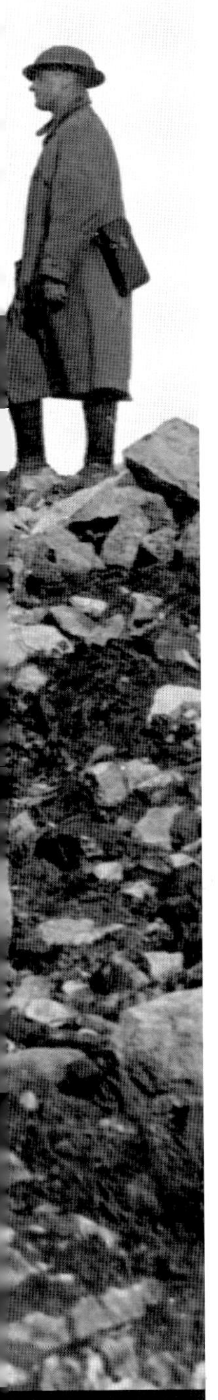

A HUMAN TRAGEDY

World War I was one of the greatest tragedies the world had experienced. In just over four years of fighting, the degree of violence and death was staggering. For the Central powers, approximately 1.8 million German soldiers died, along with 1.2 million Austro-Hungarians, 325,000 Turks, and 88,000 Bulgarians. Total casualties for the four nations, including killed, wounded, and prisoners/missing, were nearly 38 million. For the Allies, approximately 1.7 million Russians, 1.4 million French, 908,000 British and British Empire, 336,000 Romanians, and 117,000 Americans perished. Total casualties for all Allied powers numbered more than 22 million. The worldwide death toll of all countries involved in the war was approximately 8.5 million soldiers.[1]

These figures do not even consider the number of civilians killed in the war. One estimate maintains 950,000 died from actual military action, while nearly 5.9 million perished from hunger and disease.[2]

THE SUFFERINGS OF WAR

Many of the soldiers who survived the war's brutality faced great hardship. Injuries from shrapnel, artillery, and mines permanently crippled and disfigured an entire generation of young men. One of the most common casualties was limbs: arms and legs shattered or maimed in combat. Doctors often had to amputate the damaged limb to save a life or prevent infection. Infection itself could cause death. Hundreds of thousands of soldiers with amputations were fitted with artificial limbs. In the United Kingdom alone, roughly 240,000 soldiers wore prostheses.[3]

The emotional wounds soldiers endured were equally devastating. The physical and psychological strain of warfare led to a type of nervous breakdown known as shell shock, what today is identified as post-traumatic stress disorder (PTSD). In severe cases, this emotional illness affected the sufferer's ability to move and function normally. Victims shook and twitched and had difficulty walking a straight line. In less extreme cases, men suffered severe anxiety, stomach cramps, and terrible nightmares. By the end of World War I, the British army reported it had handled more than 80,000 cases of shell shock.[4] Tens of thousands more cases went unreported.

The mass movement of troops and civilians across continents created ideal conditions for widespread disease. As the war was ending, a strain of influenza called the Spanish Flu swept the world. In the United States, the disease was first seen in March 1918 among troops at Fort Funston in Kansas. The soldiers did not get very sick, suffering mainly fever and chills. By August 1918, however, a more powerful strain of the virus appeared in locations thousands of miles apart: Freetown, Sierra Leone, in West Africa; Brest, France; and Boston, Massachusetts, in the United States. Brest

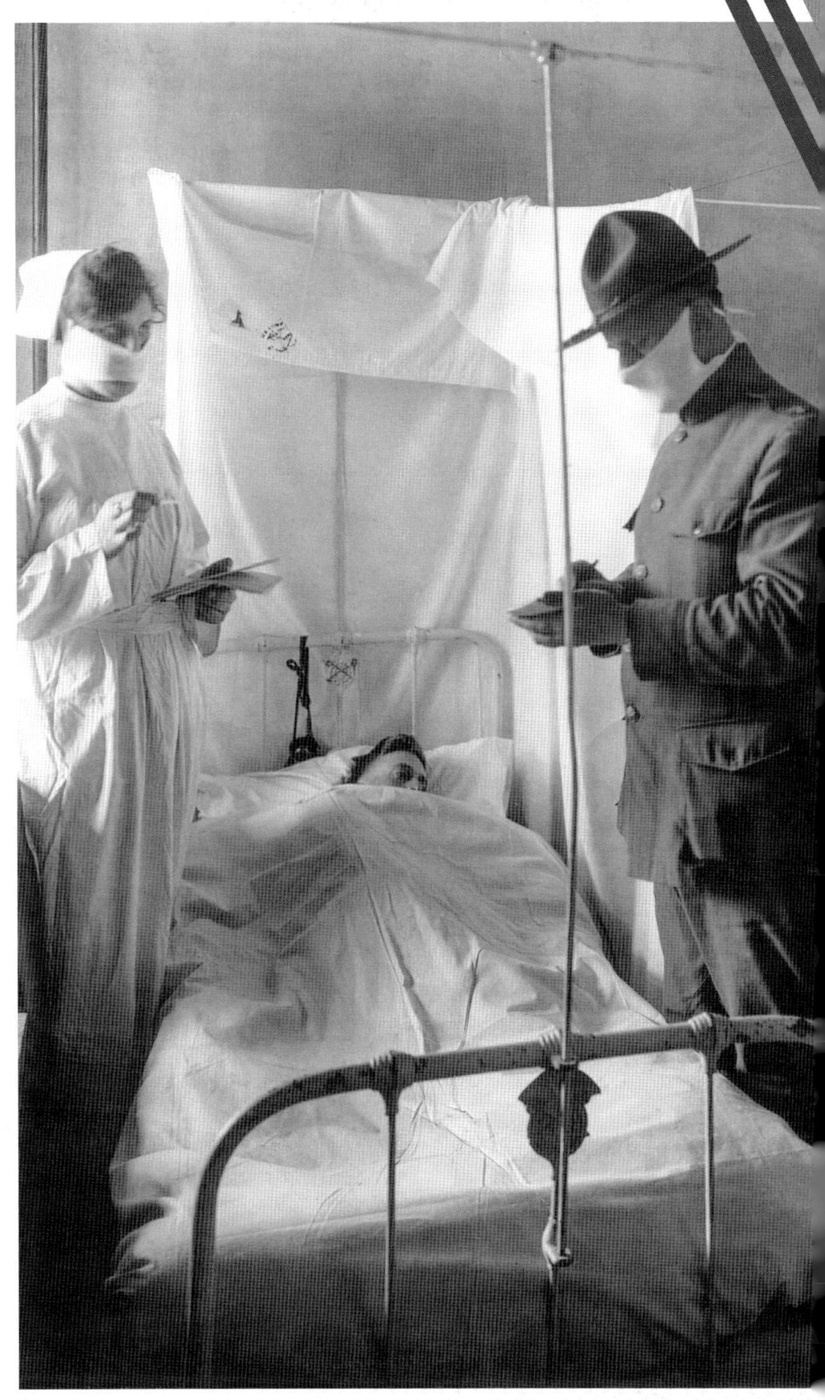

Troop movements contributed to the spread of influenza.

and Boston were both important ports from which American troops were sent to other destinations.

The disease—which had no cure—spread rapidly among US troops at home and in Europe. Many victims died within hours of becoming sick. Others died after several days. Of all US Army deaths in 1918, 60 percent were caused by the Spanish Flu.[5] The disease took a devastating toll on all frontline troops. At first, German commander Ludendorff thought the flu in the Allied armies would save his weakening forces. The virus, however, moved east into German territory. Ludendorff ultimately blamed the disease for the failure of Germany's Spring Offensive in 1918.

The flu spread like wildfire. Roughly one-third of the world's population—approximately 500 million people—was infected by the disease, resulting in 50 million deaths.[6] By early 1921, the Spanish Flu had disappeared as mysteriously as it had arrived.

SCORCHED EARTH

Four years of intense fighting took a ferocious toll on the landscape. Roads, farms, and entire villages were laid waste, nearly wiped from the earth. Bridges, railroads, and canals were destroyed beyond use. Forests and woods were splintered apart by artillery shelling, mortars, and rifle fire.

The trenches of the western front along the once-pastoral regions of France and Belgium appeared like an ugly scar on the land. "The earth was churned up so ferociously that it took on the form of a sea of mud that seemed to have no beginning or end," wrote one observer.[7] Gruesomely, thousands of bodies remained buried where they fell.

Europe's soldiers and civilians returning to their battered communities took on the dangerous task of cleaning up the battlefields. The fields had to be cleared of weapons, ammunition, vehicles, thousands of miles of barbed wire, soldiers' personal belongings, and other wartime debris. Trenches, tunnels, and craters had to be filled in with earth and concrete bunkers and pillboxes demolished and carted away.

RELICS FROM THE PAST

Belgian and French authorities are still cleaning up the remains of World War I battlefields. Called Iron Harvests, military workers continue to dig up tons of munitions, including toxic chemicals used in gas warfare. In 2011, Belgian and French harvests recovered 274 short tons (250 metric tons) of munitions. Sometimes a large weapons depot is discovered—in 2004, 3,000 German artillery shells were found in a single spot. Since the war ended, exploding World War I munitions around Ypres have killed more than 350 people.[8] Many of the victims have been farmers plowing the land with heavy tractors. When collection teams find a shell, they place it in a crate with an antitank mine and an explosive. The crates are buried in holes 13 feet (4 m) deep and covered with earth. Then the crates are exploded one by one. Shells containing mustard gas or phosgene are drained and destroyed.

At the end of the war, recently dead bodies and soldiers' graves dotted the battlefields along the western front. The British army's Directorate of Graves Registration & Enquiries (DGR&E) and the British War Graves Commission (IWGC) handled the problem of locating isolated graves, organizing cemeteries, and locating the missing men, estimated at 500,000.[9] Thousands of British and French volunteers performed the difficult work. Bodies were recovered and properly reburied, while many small cemeteries were dug up and combined into larger ones. The remains of many thousands were found but never identified.

THE COST OF WAR

Various estimates place the money spent on World War I at roughly $200 billion, in 1914–1918 money.[10] The worldwide economic impact of the Great War, however, can never be accurately tallied.

Millions of Europeans were killed, disabled, and seriously wounded. Many of the victims were young men of working age. The destruction of farms, industries, small businesses, and communication and transportation systems severely damaged many European economies. Many people were thrust into poverty with little hope of relief. In Austria, agricultural production dropped significantly, and starvation was widespread. Inflation skyrocketed throughout Europe and in Russia.

Under the punishing financial terms of the Treaty of Versailles, which ended the war, Germany especially suffered. Inflation and the oppressive reparations the treaty imposed damaged Germany's economy. The personal savings of the middle class were wiped out, and widespread unemployment soared. The economic crisis led to violence and social unrest, paving the way for the rise of Adolf Hitler's Nazi Party in the 1930s and World War II (1939–1945).

World War I began with an assassination and the expectation that fighting would end in a matter of months. Instead, millions died, entire nations lay devastated, and economies were left in ruins. Four empires—Russian, German, Austro-Hungarian, and Ottoman—had toppled, and with them their rulers. The maps of Europe and the Middle East were redrawn.

World War I's greatest legacy was what it failed to accomplish—a lasting peace. Despite the efforts of international leaders, the world was at war again in 1939—suffering even greater destruction and loss of life.

THE TREATY OF VERSAILLES

War between the Allied powers and Germany officially ended with the signing of the Treaty of Versailles on June 28, 1919. Under the terms of the treaty, Germany gave the territory of Alsace-Lorraine back to France, surrendered eastern districts to Poland, and turned over several territories to Belgium, Lithuania, and Denmark. The German military was reduced to very low levels and not allowed to have certain classes of heavy weapons. Germany was also made to pay reparations to the Allies for the losses and damages they suffered during the war. The German government believed the conditions of the treaty were too harsh and signed it under protest.

TIMELINE

June 28, 1914

Archduke Franz Ferdinand, heir to the Austro-Hungarian throne, is assassinated.

September 1914

The first battle of the Marne is fought.

January 1915

Germans launch the first Zeppelin raids on the United Kingdom.

April 22–May 25, 1915

The second battle of Ypres is fought, featuring the first use of poison gas.

July 1, 1916

The battle of the Somme begins; it ends in November with no decisive winner.

April 6, 1917

The United States declares war on Germany.

July 1917

The third battle of Ypres (Passchendaele) begins.

November 20, 1917

The battle of Cambrai begins, featuring the first large-scale use of tanks.

April 25, 1915

Allied forces land on Gallipoli.

May 7, 1915

The British liner *Lusitania* is sunk by a German U-boat.

February 21, 1916

The battle of Verdun begins.

May 31, 1916

The battle of Jutland between the British Grand Fleet and the German navy begins.

June 6, 1918

US Marines begin the fight at the battle of Belleau Wood, part of the German Spring Offensive.

September 12, 1918

Americans attack the Germans at Saint-Mihiel.

September 1918

The Allies launch the Meuse-Argonne Offensive.

November 11, 1918

Germany signs the armistice, officially ending World War I.

ESSENTIAL FACTS

KEY PLAYERS

- German generals Paul von Hindenburg and Erich Ludendorff won major victories over the Russians.
- American general John J. Pershing commanded the American Expeditionary Forces (AEF).
- Kaiser Wilhelm II led Germany during World War I.
- Woodrow Wilson was president of the United States during World War I.

KEY STATISTICS

- More than 65 million soldiers from five continents fought in World War I.
- Approximately 8.5 million soldiers and 5 million civilians were killed.
- Casualties at the four-month battle of the Somme totaled more than one million killed, wounded, and missing.
- Combatants spent approximately $200 billion on war costs.

IMPACT ON HISTORY

Politically, the war resulted in the downfall of four major empires: the German, Austro-Hungarian, Russian, and Ottoman. It also contributed to the Bolshevik Revolution in Russia, and the subsequent rise of communism in that nation and beyond. Economically, the war disrupted European economies, paving the way for the United States to become the world's leading industrial power. World War I witnessed the deaths of more soldiers and civilians than any previous war in history. The armistice failed to bring lasting peace. The agreement's punishing conditions, shouldered primarily by Germany, set the stage for the rise of German Nazism and the outbreak of World War II only 20 years later.

QUOTE

"Humanity . . . must be mad to do what it is doing. . . . What scenes of horror and carnage! . . . Hell cannot be so terrible."

—Diary of a French Lieutenant, May 23, 1916

GLOSSARY

ALLIANCE
A formal agreement between nations.

ARMISTICE
A temporary stop of fighting by mutual agreement.

ARTILLERY
Large guns manned by a crew of operators used to shoot long distances.

BOMBARD
To attack with bombs, shells, or other explosives.

CATACLYSMIC
Possessing the qualities of a great upheaval or disaster.

CIVILIAN
A person not serving in the armed forces.

FLANK
The right or left side of a military formation.

FRONT
An area where a battle is taking place.

HOWITZER
A short cannon that fires shells in a high curving path.

MOBILIZE
To become prepared for war.

MORTAR
A front-loaded cannon used to fire shells in a high arc.

PILLBOX
A small concrete structure for machine guns or other weapons.

RECONNAISSANCE
An exploration of an area to gather information about the activity of military forces.

REPARATION
Compensation required from a defeated nation for damage or injury during a war.

SHRAPNEL
Shell fragments from an exploded shell.

ADDITIONAL RESOURCES

SELECTED BIBLIOGRAPHY

Barton, Peter. *The Battlefields of the First World War: The Unseen Panoramas of the Western Front*. London: Constable, 2005. Print.

Halpern, Paul G. *A Naval History of World War I*. Annapolis, MD: Naval Institute, 1994. Print.

Hart, Peter. *The Great War: A Combat History of the First World War*. New York: Oxford UP, 2013. Print.

Willmott, H. P. *World War I*. New York: Dorling Kindersley, 2009. Print.

FURTHER READINGS

Atwood, Kathryn J. *Women Heroes of World War I: 16 Remarkable Resistors, Soldiers, Spies, and Medics*. Chicago: Chicago Review, 2014. Print.

Kenney, Karen Latchana. *Everything World War I*. Washington, DC: National Geographic Society, 2014. Print.

Pratt, Mary K. *World War I*. Minneapolis: ABDO, 2014. Print.

Vander Hook, Sue. *The United States Enters World War I*. Minneapolis: ABDO, 2010. Print.

WEBSITES

To learn more about Essential Library of World War I, visit **booklinks.abdopublishing.com**. These links are routinely monitored and updated to provide the most current information available.

PLACES TO VISIT

National World War I Museum at Liberty Memorial
100 W. Twenty-Sixth Street
Kansas City, MO 64108
816-888-8100
https://theworldwar.org/explore/collections
The museum houses more than 75,000 artifacts telling the story of the Great War from the beginning to the Armistice.

Old Rhinebeck Aerodrome
9 Norton Road
Red Hook, NY 12571
845-752-3200
http://oldrhinebeck.org/ORA/
The museum features original World War I aircraft from the United States, the United Kingdom, Germany, France, and Italy. Dogfights are performed every Sunday, from June through October.

World War I Historical Association (WWIHA)
2625 Alcatraz Avenue, #237
Berkeley, CA 94705-2702
http://ww1ha.org/the-first-world-war/
The WWIHA offers books, lectures, and annual events to promote interest in the war and preserve the memory of those who served their nations.

SOURCE NOTES

CHAPTER 1. SEEDS OF DISCONTENT

1. "WWI Casualty and Death Tables." *PBS*. PBS, n.d. Web. 16 July 2015.

2. Martin Gilbert. *The First World War: A Complete History.* New York: Holt, 1994. Print. xv.

3. John Keegan. *The First World War.* New York: Knopf, 1999. Print. 3.

4. Eric Brose. "Arms Race Prior to 1913, Armament Policy." *1914–1918 Online. International Encyclopedia of the First World War.* Freie Universität Berlin, 15 July 2015. Web. 16 July 2015.

5. "Heir to Austria's Throne Is Slain with His Wife by a Bosnian Youth to Avenge Seizure of His Country." *New York Times.* New York Times, 29 June 1914. Web. 16 July 2015.

6. Martin Gilbert. *The First World War: A Complete History.* New York: Holt, 1994. Print. 26.

7. Ibid.

CHAPTER 2. 1914: STORM CLOUDS BREAK

1. Anthony Livesey. *Great Battles of World War I.* New York: Macmillan, 1989. Print. 16.

2. "Battle of Tannenberg: 26–30 August 1914." *BBC History*. BBC, 2014. Web. 16 July 2015.

3. Ibid.

4. "The War in the Air." *First World War*. Michael Duffy, 22 Aug. 2009. Web. 16 July 2015.

5. H. P. Willmott. *World War I.* New York: Dorling Kindersley, 2009. Print. 56.

6. S. L. A. Marshall. *The American Heritage History of World War I.* New York: American Heritage/Bonanza, 1982. Print. 77.

7. "Life in the Trenches." *First World War.* Michael Duffy, 22 Aug. 2009. Web. 16 July 2015.

CHAPTER 3. 1915: THE CONFLICT SPREADS

1. Anthony Livesey. *Great Battles of World War I.* New York: Macmillan, 1989. Print. 56.

2. Ibid. 54.

3. Ibid. 57.

4. H. P. Willmott. *World War I.* New York: Dorling Kindersley, 2009. Print. 81.

5. John Keegan. *The First World War.* New York: Knopf, 1999. Print. 248.

6. S. L. A. Marshall. *The American Heritage History of World War I.* New York: American Heritage/Bonanza, 1982. Print. 107.

7. Peter Hart. *The Great War: A Combat History of the First World War.* New York: Oxford UP, 2013. Print. 144.

8. Ibid. 140.

CHAPTER 4. 1916: THE BIG PUSH

1. "Winter Battle of the Masurian Lakes Begins." *History*. A&E Television, 2015. Web. 16 July 2015.

2. H. P. Willmott. *World War I*. New York: Dorling Kindersley, 2009. Print. 138.

3. Anthony Livesey. *Great Battles of World War I*. New York: Macmillan, 1989. Print. 68.

4. John Keegan. *The First World War*. New York: Knopf, 1999. Print. 280.

5. H. P. Willmott. *World War I*. New York: Dorling Kindersley, 2009. Print. 139.

6. Anthony Livesey. *Great Battles of World War I*. New York: Macmillan, 1989. Print. 72.

7. S. L. A. Marshall. *The American Heritage History of World War I*. New York: American Heritage/Bonanza, 1982. Print. 185.

8. "Battle of Verdun." *Encyclopedia Britannica*. Encyclopedia Britannica, 2015. Web. 16 July 2015.

9. S. L. A. Marshall. *The American Heritage History of World War I*. New York: American Heritage/Bonanza, 1982. Print. 176.

10. John Campbell. *Jutland—An Analysis of the Fighting*. New York: Lyons, 1998. *The World War I Document Archive*. Web. 16 July 2015.

11. John Keegan. *The First World War*. New York: Knopf, 1999. Print. 274.

12. A. A. Hoehling. *The Great War at Sea: A History of Naval Action, 1914–1918*. New York: Crowell, 1965. Print. 86.

13. "The Battle of the Somme—1916." *First World War*. Michael Duffy, 22 Aug. 2009. Web. 16 July 2015.

14. H. P. Willmott. *World War I*. New York: Dorling Kindersley, 2009. Print. 149.

15. John Keegan. *The First World War*. New York: Knopf, 1999. Print. 306.

16. H. P. Willmott. *World War I*. New York: Dorling Kindersley, 2009. Print. 161.

17. Spencer Tucker, ed. *Encyclopedia of World War I*. Santa Barbara, CA: ABC-CLIO. Print. 1153.

18. William Philpott. "Somme, Battles of." *1914–1918 Online. International Encyclopedia of the First World War*. Freie Universität Berlin, 15 July 2015. Web. 16 July 2015.

19. "Tanks." *First World War*. Michael Duffy, 22 Aug. 2009. Web. 16 July 2015.

SOURCE NOTES CONTINUED

CHAPTER 5. 1917: THE CRITICAL YEAR

1. "The Second Battle of the Aisne, 1917." *First World War*. Michael Duffy, 22 Aug. 2009. Web. 16 July 2015.

2. "Nivelle Offensive Ends in Failure." *History*. A&E Television, 2015. Web. 16 July 2015.

3. "The Battle of Messines—1917." *First World War*. Michael Duffy, 22 Aug. 2009. Web. 16 July 2015.

4. Anthony Livesey. *Great Battles of World War I*. New York: Macmillan, 1989. Print. 119.

5. Ibid. 120.

6. Ibid. 130.

7. "The Third Battle of Ypres—1917." *First World War*. Michael Duffy, 22 Aug. 2009. Web. 16 July 2015.

8. Anthony Livesey. *Great Battles of World War I*. New York: Macmillan, 1989. Print. 149.

9. "The Battle of Cambrai." *First World War*. Michael Duffy, 22 Aug. 2009. Web. 16 July 2015.

10. Ibid.

11. Woodrow Wilson. "Joint Address to Congress Leading to a Declaration of War Against Germany (1917)." *Ourdocuments.gov*. National Archives, n.d. Web. 16 July 2015.

12. S. L. A. Marshall. *The American Heritage History of World War I*. New York: American Heritage/Bonanza, 1982. Print. 250.

CHAPTER 6. THE WAR IN THE AIR

1. Anthony Livesey. *Great Battles of World War I*. New York: Macmillan, 1989. Print. 133.

2. Ibid. 140.

3. Arch Whitehouse. *The Zeppelin Fighters*. Garden City, NY: Doubleday, 1966. Print. 146–150.

4. Anthony Livesey. *Great Battles of World War I*. New York: Macmillan, 1989. Print. 140.

5. Trevor Nevitt Dupuy. *The War in the Air*. New York: Franklin Watts, 1967. Print. 50.

6. S. L. A. Marshall. *The American Heritage History of World War I*. New York: American Heritage/Bonanza, 1982. Print. 322.

7. Trevor Nevitt Dupuy. *The War in the Air*. New York: Franklin Watts, 1967. Print. 71.

8. "The Battle of Arras and Bloody April." *World War I Aviation*. William Ira Boucher, 24 May 2014. Web. 16 July 2015.

9. "American Legion Post 85 Post History." *American Legion Post 85*. American Legion, n.d. Web. 16 July 2015.

10. Evan Andrews. "6 Famous WWI Fighter Aces." *History*. A&E Television, 22 May 2014. Web. 16 July 2015.

CHAPTER 7. 1918: THE TIDE TURNS

1. Richard Holmes. *The Western Front*. New York: TV, 2000. Print. 198.

2. H. P. Willmott. *World War I*. New York: Dorling Kindersley, 2009. Print. 256.

3. Dennis E. Showalter. "World War I." *Encyclopedia Britannica*. Encyclopedia Britannica, 2015. Web. 16 July 2015.

4. J. Rickard. "Battle of Cantigny." *HistoryofWar.org*. History of War, 10 Aug. 2007. Web. 16 July 2015.

5. H. P. Willmott. *World War I*. New York: Dorling Kindersley, 2009. Print. 282.

6. Jean Ebbert and Marie-Beth Hall. *The First, the Few, the Forgotten: Navy and Marine Corps Women in World War I*. Annapolis, MD: Naval Institute, 2002. Print. ix.

CHAPTER 8. A HUMAN TRAGEDY

1. "WWI Casualty and Death Tables." *PBS*. PBS, n.d. Web. 16 July 2015.

2. Peter Hart. *The Great War: A Combat History of the First World War*. New York: Oxford UP, 2013. Print. 468.

3. Jennifer Llewellyn, et al. "The Human Cost of World War I." *Alpha History*. Alpha History, 2014. Web. 16 July 2015.

4. Joanna Bourke. "Shell Shock during World War One." *BBC*. BBC, 10 Mar. 2011. Web. 16 July 2015.

5. Alan Axelrod. *The Complete Idiot's Guide to World War I*. Indianapolis, IN: Alpha, 2000. Print. 358–359.

6. Jeffery K. Taubenberger and David M. Morens. "The Mother of All Pandemics." *Emerging Infectious Diseases* 12.1 (2006): 15. *CDC.gov*. Web. 16 July 2015.

7. Matthew Leonard. "Muddy Hell." *Modern Conflict Archaeology*. Modern Conflict Archaeology, n.d. Web. 16 July 2015.

8. Martin Fletcher. "Lethal Relics from World War I Are Still Emerging." *Telegraph*. Telegraph Media Group, 12 July 2013. Web. 16 July 2015.

9. Peter Hodgkinson. "Clearing the Dead." *Centre for First World War Studies* 3.1 (Sept. 2007). *Virtual Library*. Web. 16 July 2015.

10. "Aftermath." *The First World War*. National Archives, n.d. Web. 16 July 2015.

INDEX

ABOUT THE AUTHOR

Nel Yomtov is an award-winning author of nonfiction books and graphic novels for young readers. His writing passions include history, geography, military, nature, sports, biographies, and careers. Yomtov has also written, edited, and colored hundreds of Marvel comic books. Nel has served as editorial director of a children's nonfiction book publisher and as executive editor of Hammond World Atlas book division. Nel lives in the New York City area with his wife.